THE TAG

RABINDRANATH TAGORE
(*From the portrait by S. K. Hesh*)

THE TAGORE BIRTHDAY BOOK

(SELECTED FROM THE ENGLISH WORKS OF RABINDRANATH TAGORE)

Edited by
C.F. ANDREWS

Rupa . Co

Published 2002 by

Rupa & Co

7/16, Ansari Road, Daryaganj,
New Delhi 110 002

Sales Centres:

Allahabad Bangalore Chandigarh Chennai
Dehradun Hyderabad Jaipur Kathmandu
Kolkata Ludhiana Mumbai Pune

ISBN 81-7167-733-9

Printed in India by
Rekha Printers Pvt Ltd, A-102/1,
Okhla Industrial Area,
Phase-II, New Delhi-110 020

THE POET'S DEDICATION

WHO are you, reader, reading my poems an hundred years hence ?

I cannot send you one single flower from this wreath of the spring, one single streak of gold from yonder clouds.

Open your doors and look abroad.

From your blossoming garden gather fragrant memories of the vanished flowers of an hundred years before.

In the joy of your heart may you feel the living joy, that sang one spring morning sending its glad voice across an hundred years.

Gardener.

LIST OF ILLUSTRATIONS

PREFACE

I AM writing this brief preface, in the first place in order to thank Heimanti, Dinshaw, Amiyo, and Dhiren, my young enthusiastic companions, for the invaluable help they have given me in the delightful task of arranging this Birthday Book of the poet whom we love.

Secondly, it may be necessary to explain to Western readers that throughout the natural imagery used by Rabindranath Tagore, there runs an echo of some human mood of joy, or pain, or wistful longing; because in Eastern poetry man is intimately associated with nature.

Thus such simple words of a song as 'The swan has taken its flight to the lake beyond the mountains', or 'I have reached the brink of the shoreless sea', have an inner meaning, which must be looked for, besides the literal meaning. There is also a deep religious significance attached to much that is written. In this, the first personal pronoun constantly refers to the soul, while the second person refers to God. For instance, in Tagore's translation of Kabir's Poems we read:

'From the beginning to the ending of time there is love between thee and me: and how shall such love be extinguished?

'As the river enters into the ocean, so my heart touches thee.'

The border-line between the human and the divine love is often difficult to trace, and both meanings are frequently included. For this reason I have avoided as far as possible the use of a capital letter when a pronoun refers to the divine name. In this respect I have followed the example of the English Bible.

One further point needs a slight notice. In Northern India the long drought is broken by the monsoon in June and July. The rain, therefore, has a gracious beauty of its own, and often brings to the mind tender, thoughtful imaginations of a sadness which is also sweet.

Many of those who read this volume, or use it for collecting autographs from friends, will like to know that the poet's own birthday, as far as can be reckoned in a Western calendar, comes about May 6 each year. At Santiniketan it is kept by the children with music, drama, and song.

The one great wish present with us all, during the months in which this book was being arranged, has been that it may be widely used to scatter a gleam of sunshine over the earth and to bring the East and the West nearer together in love.

C. F. ANDREWS.

SANTINIKETAN.

THE LIFE AND WRITINGS OF RABINDRANATH TAGORE

(*a*) HIS LIFE

A BRIEF account of Rabindranath Tagore's life, together with a description of the most important of his writings, will help the reader who uses this volume to understand the references and to appreciate the poet, whose songs are quoted in this Calendar.

Rabindranath Tagore was born in Calcutta on May 6, 1861. He was the grandson of Prince Dwarkanath Tagore, who was one of the most enlightened intellectual leaders of Bengal more than a century ago. The eldest son of the Prince was named Debendranath Tagore. He became universally known and loved throughout India, receiving the venerable title 'Maharshi', which means, when translated, 'Great Saint'.

The poet was the youngest son of Maharshi. His mother died when he was quite young. From childhood onwards a love of solitude and peace became natural to the young child, and he grew up with a deeply sensitive and imaginative nature.

The story of his childhood was told to me in the following words, which I have often repeated :

'I was very lonely—that was the chief feature of my childhood. My father I saw very seldom : he was away a great deal, but his presence pervaded the whole house, and was one of the deepest influences on my life. Kept in charge of the servants after my mother died, I used to sit, day after day, in front of the window and picture to myself what was going on in the outer world. From the very first time I can remember, I was passionately fond of Nature. . . . I had such an exceeding love for Nature, I cannot tell how to describe it to you: but Nature was a kind of loving companion always with me, and always revealing to me some fresh beauty.'

His illumination as a poet came to him when he was eighteen, and his writings began afterwards to pour forth in profuse abundance. They were chiefly of a lyrical character, and some of his most beautiful Bengali poems were written at this early stage of his long life as a poet.

His father sent him to do practical work among the village people at Shileida, on the banks of the River Padma. He was married, and had five children, two sons and three daughters. The Padma River is one of the branches of the Ganges, as it divides into a delta near the sea. The young poet's love of solitude had full scope here, even in the midst of an active married life; for he used to retire from time to time and live, for months together, alone in a house-boat moored to the sand flats in the midst of the river. He kept at other times in closest touch with the villagers owing to his practical work. During the twenty years, from 1880 to 1900, he composed not only his lyrical poems, but also dramas, short stories, and novels, which have made him famous in Bengali literature as a master of prose as well as the greatest Indian poet of his age.

But when the twentieth century dawned, he became restless, and knew for certain that a time of change had been reached. In the end, amid many financial difficulties, he founded his school at Santiniketan, where his father, Maharshi, had long ago retired for meditation. Here, Rabindranath Tagore settled down to teach the young children who gathered round him. In his school method, he avoided as much as possible all formal and conventional teaching, and adopted new and living personal ways of inspiring a keen desire for learning among his pupils. He also taught his children to love the open-air life in the midst of nature. This school has now become world-famous on account of its advanced and progressive educational character.

But while the school flourished under the poet's fostering care, his own life underwent a great change. This was almost equivalent to a second spiritual birth. For in a brief space of time his own loved wife died and also his youngest daughter. Then followed the third crowning sorrow in the death, owing to cholera, of his youngest son, who was already showing signs of wonderful poetic genius, not unlike his father's. Yet out of the depth of all this suffering there came to the poet himself a new sense of the fullness and beauty of human life. He has expressed this in *Gitanjali*, where he writes:

'O thou last fulfilment of life, Death, my death, come and whisper to me!

'Day after day have I kept watch for thee: for thee have I borne the joys and pangs of life.

'All that I am, that I have, that I hope, and all my love have ever flowed towards thee in depth of secrecy.

'One final glance from thine eyes and my life will be ever thine own.'

The poet visited England in the year 1912, after a prolonged illness. He went there in the first place in order to undergo a very serious operation; but this visit unexpectedly opened to him the door of the West. His own English translations of his Bengali poems began now to appear. These, while still in manuscript and unpublished, had attracted the attention of the Irish poet, W. B. Yeats, who wrote about them as follows:

'I have carried the manuscript of these translations about with me for days, reading it in railway trains, or on the top of omnibuses and in restaurants, and I have often had to close it lest some stranger would see how much it moved me. These lyrics display in their thought a world I have dreamed of all my life long.'

After his visit to Europe and America in 1912 and 1913, and the award of the Nobel Prize for World Literature, Rabindranath Tagore's life gradually widened out towards a larger horizon, embracing all humanity. His heart has been drawn more and more towards the solution of the new problem of the meeting of the races of the world together in mutual harmony and love. He has also sought means for the removal of the alarming evil of growing colour prejudice. This latter appeared to him to be one of the worst portents of the modern age, afflicting mankind. He wrote to me in the year 1913:

'This race problem is I believe the one burning question of the present age; and we must be prepared to go through the martyrdom of suffering and humiliation till the victory of God in man is achieved.'

Tagore's three philosophical works in English, called *Sadhana*, *Personality*, and *Creative Unity*, were written during these years. They have the thought of universal humanity in view. His poems contained in *Fruit-Gathering* and *Crossing* strike the same note of the gradual coming into being of the one Nation of Man. This is explained in a concrete manner in *Nationalism*. His translations of Kabir's poems, from which I have freely quoted, express the same thought. Very often, beneath the simple imagery taken from Nature, this deeper philosophy of human life is represented in poetic form. Such a phrase, for instance, as

'Have you not heard the notes which the Unstruck Music is playing?'

may be referred to this harmony in Man which is being

slowly reached by the power of the divine urge from within.

Rabindranath Tagore has now reached old age. He is nearly seventy years old. His health of late has been very greatly impaired, but his ardent lovers and admirers all over the world will earnestly pray that his life may be prolonged, in God's providence, for further blessing to mankind.

(*b*) HIS WRITINGS

(1) Poems

Gitanjali.—This was the first volume of poems in English that Rabindranath Tagore ever published in the West. They are written in rhythmical prose, and have all the qualities of true poetry, though composed without rhyme or metre. The book contains translations from Bengali poems, which were written during the time of his great bereavement after the death of his wife and his two youngest children. About these poems he told me on one occasion: 'I composed them in solitude during my sorrow without any idea of publication. They were written for myself: but since I found them to be a spiritual help to others, I consented to publish them in Bengali. At a later time, on my voyage to England, when I was convalescent after serious illness, I began to translate them into very halting English.'

He gave these translations into my hands,—after he had shown them to the Irish poet, W. B. Yeats,—asking me to correct their 'faults'. But when I read the MSS., I found his English style not only chaste in its simplicity, but also perfect in its rhythm and music. It represented something unique in English literature.

Such poems as these naturally lend themselves for quotation in this Calendar, and I have used them very freely indeed. It should be remembered that by far the greater number of these songs have a deep religious significance.

They symbolise the soul's communion with God and not merely human love. Quotations from *Gitanjali* in this book must be specially studied in this deeper spiritual sense.

The Gardener.—This second series of poems was published soon after *Gitanjali*, and won an almost equal place in public esteem. They represent the more purely human aspects of love. It may be stated that these two books of the poet—along with the *Crescent Moon* and *Sadhana*—have had the largest reading public during the past fifteen years, both in England and in America. Each fresh generation of readers seems to discover anew their beauty.

The Crescent Moon.—Tagore's child-poems have been universally recognised as delightful and original. It is noticeable that English and American readers have found them as charming in their English setting as Indian readers have found them in their Bengali metre and in Indian translations. These poems of childhood have also won their place in most European and Eastern literatures. It would be difficult to find a better example of the community of sentiment about children prevalent in every country of the world. It is clear that both the humour and the beauty of childhood are the same all the world over, and the poet has been able to touch the human heart everywhere by these simple poems about little children.

Lover's Gift and Crossing.—These two collections of the poet's songs have been bound up in one volume. They represent together the springtime and the autumn of life. In the later portion of the book, some of the poems written during the World War have been inserted.

Fruit-Gathering.—The poet, in this collection, has gathered together many of the songs that remained over after the publication of *Gitanjali*. *Fruit-Gathering* may thus be regarded in a certain measure as a sequel to *Gitanjali*. One of the greatest poems in this volume is called 'The Oarsmen'. In this he urges mankind to adventure forth into the unknown, leaving behind the desolate past. This and other poems were composed during the War period.

The Fugitive.—Songs of great delicacy and beauty are contained in this collection, which was the last to be published by the poet. They often represent a slight passing mood which reveals the hidden depths of personality. Some translations are included from the 'Baul' poets of India, who have a simple religious philosophy of their own of singular beauty. There are also dramatic scenes interspersed; the different subjects of these are taken from the ancient epics.

(2) Dramas

Chitra.—This was the first of the poet's dramas to be translated by his own hand into English. It is the most purely classical of all his writings both in its form and language. The play depicts the ideal Woman, in her physical perfection and also in her spiritual devotion for love's sake.

The Post Office.—Among the poet's dramas, which are acted by his own boys at Santiniketan, this is most often chosen. It portrays a sick child, who sits at the window and greets the different passers-by while he waits for a letter from the King.

The Cycle of Spring.—In its original Bengali setting, this drama is replete with music and songs. It is the Drama of Spring. The young band of adventurers, in the play, go out to find the Old Man and to capture him. The Old Man typifies Winter and Death. But in the dramatic setting he is found to be the same as Youth and Springtime. Thus this is one of the 'mystery' plays of Tagore, where the secret of the play is kept well hidden until the climax is reached. It is also a great favourite for the boys and girls at Santiniketan to perform on the open-air stage. But very much depends upon the Bengali music.

The King of the Dark Chamber.—This second 'mystery' play of the poet has here been translated into English. The King of the Dark Chamber remains ever unseen, but he directs and guides his kingdom from within. The interest of the play centres in the character of Sudarshana, the Queen.

Sacrifice.—Four complete plays are contained in this one volume. The most celebrated of them is called 'Sacrifice', after which the book is named. These four plays are classical in form, and are written in stately, rhythmical prose. They are suitable for amateur acting. 'Sacrifice' has frequently been performed in England and America.

Red Oleanders.—This is one of the more recent of Rabindranath Tagore's dramas. It is a modern play, both in its language and spirit. The poet condemns the mechanical civilisation which has arisen in modern times and has destroyed everywhere the pure beauty of Nature. It is a very powerful appeal,—akin to *Nationalism* among his prose works for its denunciation of the ugliness and inhumanity of the modern age.

(3) Epigrams

Stray Birds.—Two volumes of epigrams have come from the poet's pen, called *Stray Birds* and *Fireflies*. Deep truths are hidden in some illustration from nature, or in some homely metaphor, or in a passing fancy. Such books naturally lend themselves for quotation in the Calendar, and I have used them freely.

Fireflies.—This second series of epigrams, written chiefly in China and Japan, has hitherto been published only in America. But it is soon to appear among the poet's works in England.

(4) Novels and Stories

Gora.—This long novel, written more than twenty years ago, is still the best known of the poet's prose writings in Bengal. It is a vivid and detailed study of Indian religious society in modern times, and it should be read by everyone who wishes intimately to understand the East.

The Home and the World.—This novel describes the modern Swadeshi (Nationalist) movement at its height in Bengal. It gives a picture of New India during its national awakening and social upheaval.

The Wreck.—This is one of the novels of Rabindranath Tagore, which has gained great praise in Bengal for its character-drawing and powers of description.

Hungry Stones.—These are some of the most famous 'Short Stories' of Tagore. Two other volumes, called *Mashi* and *Broken Ties*, have also been published in English. In Bengal itself, these intimate stories of Bengali home life are regarded as ranking very high indeed among the poet's writings.

(5) Philosophy

Sadhana.—Rabindranath Tagore first published, among his prose works in English, this new and simple account of the ancient philosophy and religious teaching of India. It has remained, for English readers, one of the most popular of his works. I have taken many quotations from it in the Calendar.

Thought Relics.—Up to the present, these beautiful prose paragraphs from the poet's Bengali writings, translated into English by himself, have not appeared in England. But an edition is likely soon to be brought out, which will follow the American edition, and also contain many new passages.

Personality.—These essays were written in Japan and America during the year 1916. They give the poet's philosophic idea of human personality. His own conception is a novel one in the West, and on that account the book has received very careful consideration.

Creative Unity.—Lectures delivered in Europe and America, during the poet's tour in 1920 and 1921, are gathered in this volume, which forms the completion of the philosophic ideas contained in *Sadhana* and *Personality.*

Nationalism.—During the World War, the poet visited

Japan and wrote these lectures there, warning Japan against the evils of militarist imperialism, which were the sinister outcome of modern civilisation in the West with its selfish creed of absolute national sovereignty. This book led to much criticism at the time, during the war fever, but the poet's main thesis has since been very widely accepted.

(6) Miscellaneous

My Reminiscences.—These represent various sketches of the poet's boyhood and youth and early manhood. They tell the story of his solitary childhood ; his illumination as a poet ; his literary career during his younger days, and his welcome by the novelist Bankim as the new leading writer of Bengal.

Glimpses of Bengal.—The homely scenery and domestic life of Bengal are depicted in this series of letters.

BENEDICTION

BLESS this little heart, this white soul, that has won the kiss of heaven for our earth.

He loves the light of the sun, he loves the sight of his mother's face.

He has not learnt to despise the dust and to hanker after gold.

Clasp him to your heart and bless him.

He has come into this land of an hundred cross-roads.

I know not how he chose you from the crowd, came to your door, and grasped your hand to ask his way.

He will follow you, laughing and talking, and not a doubt in his heart.

Keep his trust, lead him straight and bless him.

Lay your hand on his head and pray that though the waves underneath grow threatening, yet the breath from above may come to fill his sails and waft him to the haven of peace.

Forget him not in your hurry, let him come to your heart and bless him.

Crescent Moon.

WINTER

When the heart is hard and parched up, come upon me with a shower of mercy.

When grace is lost from life, come with a burst of song.

When tumultuous work raises its din on all sides shutting me out from beyond, come to me, my lord of silence, with thy peace and rest.

When my beggarly heart sits crouched, shut up in a corner, break open the door, my king, and come with the ceremony of a king.

When desire blinds the mind with delusion and dust, O thou holy one, thou wakeful, come with thy light and thy thunder.

Gitanjali.

JANUARY

Life of my life, I shall ever try to keep my body pure, knowing that thy living touch is upon all my limbs.

I shall ever try to keep all untruths out from my thoughts, knowing that thou art that truth which has kindled the light of reason in my mind.

I shall ever try to drive all evils away from my heart and keep my love in flower, knowing that thou hast thy seat in the inmost shrine of my heart.

And it shall be my endeavour to reveal thee in my actions, knowing it is thy power gives me strength to act.

Gitanjali.

JANUARY 1

JANUARY 2

January 1

The world puts off its mask of vastness to its lover. It becomes small as one song, as one kiss of the eternal.

Stray Birds.

Men are the children of light. Whenever they fully realise themselves they feel their immortality.

Personality.

The world is the ever-changing foam that floats on the surface of a sea of silence. *Fireflies.*

January 2

My heart, the bird of the wilderness, has found its sky in your eyes. Let me but soar in that sky in its lonely immensity. *Gardener.*

Man is true where he feels his infinity, where he is divine ; and the divine is the creator in him.

Personality.

In the night, when the noise is tired, the murmur of the sea fills the air, and love's play is stilled into worship.

Crossing.

January 3

January 4

January 5

January 3

The sorrowing sky has shadowed my solitude to deepen the meaning of thy touch about my heart. *Crossing.*

The perfect dawn is near, when you will mingle your life with all life and know at last your purpose. *Fruit-Gathering.*

He who is the Giver can vouchsafe a vision of the eternal in the dingiest of lanes. *Reminiscences.*

January 4

The child finds its mother when it leaves her womb. When I am parted from you, I am free to see your face. *Fruit-Gathering.*

In the drowsy dark caves of the mind dreams build their nests with fragments dropped from day's caravan. *Fireflies.*

I can feel him coming nearer and nearer, and my heart becomes glad. *Post Office.*

January 5

Love's gift is shy, it never tells its name, it flits across the shade spreading a shiver of joy along the dust. *Lover's Gift.*

My eyes strayed far and wide before I shut them and said, Here art thou. *Gitanjali.*

I have loved the sunlight, the sky and the green earth. *Crescent Moon.*

January 6

January 7

January 8

January 6

She is near to my heart as the meadow flower to the earth. *Lover's Gift.*

We truly meet God when we come to him with our offerings, and not with our wants. *Thought Relics.*

My child, the King loves you. He is coming himself. *Post Office.*

January 7

Descend at whiles from thy high audience hall. Come down amid joys and sorrows, and in my heart sing thy songs. *Creative Unity.*

The pain was great when the strings were being tuned, my Master.

Begin your music, and let me forget the pain ; let me feel in beauty what you had in your mind through these pitiless days. *Fruit-Gathering.*

I have heard the liquid murmur of the river through the darkness of midnight. *Crescent Moon.*

January 8

The world has opened its heart of light in the morning.
Come out, my heart, with thy love to meet it. *Stray Birds.*

Man's faith in God has built up all that is great in the human world. *Creative Unity.*

I know not how of a sudden my heart has flung open its doors. *Reminiscences.*

January 9

January 10

January 11

January 9

Many a glad day has come in my life. On grey mornings of rain I have crooned many an idle song.

Crescent Moon.

I love you, beloved. Forgive me, my love. Like a bird losing its way I am caught. *Gardener.*

My songs are one with my love, like the murmur of a stream. *Lover's Gift.*

January 10

Your speech is simple, my Master, but not theirs who talk of you. *Fruit-Gathering.*

Leave out my name from the gift if it be a burden, but keep my song. *Fireflies.*

Autumn sunsets have come to me at the end of a road in a lonely waste, like a bride raising her veil to accept her lover. *Crescent Moon.*

January 11

Now it is time to sit quiet, and to sing dedication of life in this silent and overflowing leisure. *Gitanjali.*

She is sweet to me as sleep is to tired limbs.

Lover's Gift.

Let not my love be a burden on you, my friend, know that it pays itself. *Fireflies.*

January 12

January 13

January 14

January 12

Man is a born child, his power is the power of growth.
Stray Birds.

Pride can never approach to where thou walkest among the poorest, the lowliest and the lost. *Gitanjali.*

Come to my garden walk, my love. Pass by the fervid flowers that press themselves on your sight.
Lover's Gift.

January 13

I am only waiting for love to give myself up at last into his hands. *Gitanjali.*

Dawn plays her lute before the gate of darkness, and is content when the sun comes out to vanish.
Fireflies.

Bless this little heart, this white soul, that has won the kiss of heaven for our earth. *Crescent Moon.*

January 14

The Lord is in me, the Lord is in you, as life is in every seed. *Kabir's Poems.*

I would be content with the smallest corner of this earth, if only she were mine. *Lover's Gift.*

He loves the light of the sun, he loves the sight of his mother's face. *Crescent Moon.*

January 15

January 16

January 17

January 15

My wishes are fools.

They shout across thy songs, my Master; let me but listen. *Stray Birds.*

This One in me knows the universe of the many. *Creative Unity.*

At the end of the stony path, in the country of virgin solitude, my friend is sitting all alone. *Gitanjali.*

January 16

My beloved is ever in my heart. That is why I see him everywhere. *King of Dark Chamber.*

Let there be flowering of love in the summer to come in the garden by the sea. *Lover's Gift.*

The echo from the depths of the Universe is reflected into our heart from the face of our beloved. *Reminiscences.*

January 17

I cannot choose the best.

The best chooses me. *Stray Birds.*

Man truly lives in the life that is beyond him. He toils for the unknown master, he stores for the unborn. *Thought Relics.*

He attains the true Name, whose words are pure, and who is free from pride and conceit. *Kabir's Poems.*

JANUARY 18

JANUARY 19

JANUARY 20

JANUARY 18

That I exist is a perpetual surprise which is life.
Stray Birds.

O woman, you are not merely the handiwork of God, but also of men. These are ever endowing you with beauty from their hearts. You are one-half woman and one-half dream. *Gardener.*

Love went forth seeking that which it knew not, leaving all it had known. *Fugitive.*

JANUARY 19

Silence will carry your voice like the nest that holds the sleeping birds. *Stray Birds.*

One day, with fresh wonder, you came into my life.
Lover's Gift.

In one salutation to thee, my God, let all my senses spread out and touch this world at thy feet. *Gitanjali.*

JANUARY 20

When I asked you to mould with my life an image from your heart for you to love, you brought your fire and force, and truth, loveliness and peace.
Fruit-Gathering.

You are like a flowering tree, amazed when I praise you for your gifts. *Fireflies.*

Let all my life take its voyage to its eternal home in one salutation to thee. *Gitanjali.*

January 21

January 22

January 23

January 21

God finds himself by creating. *Stray Birds.*

When I try to bow to thee, my obeisance cannot reach down to the depth where thy feet rest among the poorest, the lowliest and the lost. *Gitanjali.*

In love I pay my endless debt to thee for what thou art. *Fireflies.*

January 22

Your red roses carry in their burning silence all that was unutterable in me. *Lover's Gift.*

'The days pass,' Love said, 'but I wait for you.' *Fruit-Gathering.*

In the thrill of little leaves I see the air's invisible dance, and in their glimmering the secret heart-beats of the sky. *Fireflies.*

January 23

One Love it is that pervades the whole earth: few there are who know it fully. *Kabir's Poems.*

I thought I would sing love's words to their own tune, but that sounds only in my heart, and my eyes are silent.

Would you know them, friend, if there were no tune? *Fugitive.*

The first flower that blossomed on this earth was an invitation to the unborn song. *Fireflies.*

January 24

January 25

January 26

January 24

Open your door, I am waiting; the ferry of the light is done for the day.

The evening star is up. *King of Dark Chamber.*

If to-day I bring my homage to you, forgive me, my love. *Lover's Gift.*

The stream which comes from the infinite and flows towards the finite—that is the True, the Good. Its echo, which returns to the infinite, is Beauty and Joy.
Reminiscences.

January 25

Hasten, my heart, and spend yourself in love, before the day is done. *Cycle of Spring.*

I am poured forth in living notes of joy and sorrow by your breath. Should I be wholly spent in some flight of song, I shall not grieve, the tune is so dear to me.
Fugitive.

Life finds its truth and beauty, not in any exaggeration of sameness, but in harmony. *Creative Unity.*

January 26

Life finds its wealth by the claims of the world, and its worth by the claims of love. *Stray Birds.*

Let only that little be left of me whereby I may name thee my all. *Gitanjali.*

He who does good, comes to the temple gate; he who loves, reaches the shrine. *Fireflies.*

January 27

January 28

January 29

January 27

Love depends upon the will of the giver, and the poorest of the poor can indulge in such generosity.
Fugitive.

My heart is not mine to give to one only, it is given to the many. *Gardener.*

My heart beats her waves at the shore of the world and writes upon it her signature in tears with the words, 'I love thee'. *Stray Birds.*

January 28

In the dusk of the evening the bird of some early dawn comes to the nest of my silence. *Stray Birds.*

Only he helps us, who proves by his life that we have a soul whose dwelling is in the kingdom of love.
Thought Relics.

Trees are the earth's endless efforts to speak to the listening heaven. *Fireflies.*

January 29

I have only the sound of your steps to guide me in this wilderness. *Cycle of Spring.*

I shall stake all I have and when I lose my last penny I shall stake myself, and then I think I shall have won through my utter defeat. *Fruit-Gathering.*

Your eyes melt my heart as the kiss of the sun melts the snow on a mountain top. *Fugitive.*

January 30

January 31

January 30

She is dark as the longing for unknown love in the wistful night of May. *Lover's Gift.*

Our days of joy are our days of expenditure. *Thought Relics.*

God is there where the tiller is tilling the hard ground, and where the pathmaker is breaking stones. *Gitanjali.*

January 31

I came to your shore as a stranger, I lived in your house as a guest, I leave your door as a friend, my earth. *Stray Birds.*

The faith waiting in the heart of a seed promises a miracle of life, which it cannot prove at once. *Fireflies.*

The sea is beating its drums in joy, the flowers are a-tiptoe to kiss you,
For heaven is born in you, my child, in the arms of the mother-dust. *Lover's Gift.*

FEBRUARY

THE night is dark and your slumber is deep in the hush of my being.

Wake, O Pain of Love, for I know not how to open the door, and I stand outside.

The hours wait; the stars watch, the wind is still, the silence is heavy in my heart.

Wake, Love, wake! brim my empty cup and with a breath of song ruffle the night. *Fruit-Gathering.*

February 1

February 2

FEBRUARY 1

The cattle have come to their folds and birds to their nests.

Open your door : I am waiting.

King of Dark Chamber.

O my heart, let us go to that country where dwells the beloved. *Kabir's Poems.*

I wait and watch, till your shadow passes by the balcony of night, and I return with a full heart. *Fruit-Gathering.*

FEBRUARY 2

One word keep for me in thy silence, O World, when I am dead, 'I have loved'. *Stray Birds.*

My love, before the daybreak of life, you stood under some waterfall of happy dreams, filling your blood with its liquid turbulence. *Lover's Gift.*

As a river in the sea,
Work finds its fulfilment in the depth of leisure.

Fireflies.

February 3

February 4

February 5

February 3

Why should my name take such music from her tongue as to draw my heart out? *Fugitive.*

The river runs swift with a song, breaking through all barriers.

But the mountain stays and remembers and follows her with his love. *Crescent Moon.*

If you love me, beloved, forgive me my joy. Bear with my pride, beloved, and forgive me my joy. *Gardener.*

February 4

The trees, like the longings of the earth, stand-a-tiptoe to peep at the heaven. *Stray Birds.*

Truth is widowed without Love. *Fugitive.*

Like a tear or a smile, a poem is but a picture of what is taking place within. *Reminiscences.*

February 5

Woman has been man's inspiration, guiding unconsciously his restless energy. *Creative Unity.*

Man discovers his own wealth when God comes to ask gifts of him. *Fireflies.*

From fathomless depths of the eternal spring of joy the numberless sprays of laughter leap up throughout the world. *Reminiscences.*

FEBRUARY 6

FEBRUARY 7

FEBRUARY 8

February 6

Shadow, with her veil drawn, follows Light in secret meekness, with her silent steps of love. *Stray Birds.*

Eyes see only dust and earth, but feel with the heart and know pure joy. *Fugitive.*

Birth is from the mystery of night into the greater mystery of day. *Fireflies.*

February 7

Lead me in the centre of thy silence to fill my heart with songs. *Stray Birds.*

It is not the lightness of pressure in the outside world which we need in order to be free, but love which has the power to bear the world's weight, not only with ease but with joy. *Thought Relics.*

The stars are singing the love-song of the eternal.
Fruit-Gathering.

February 8

The same sun is newly born in new lands in a ring of endless dawns. *Fireflies.*

I clasp your hands and my heart plunges into the dark of your eyes. *Lover's Gift.*

Young is your life, your path long, and you drink the love we bring you at one draught and run away.
Crescent Moon.

February 9

February 10

February 11

February 9

The Father is working in his world, but the Beloved is lying asleep in our heart, in the depth of its darkness.
Thought Relics.

The spring flowers break out like the passionate pain of unspoken love. *Lover's Gift.*

This song of mine will touch your forehead like a kiss of blessing. *Crescent Moon.*

February 10

On the seashore of endless worlds children meet.
Crescent Moon.

You were in the centre of my heart, therefore when my heart wandered she never found you; you hid yourself from my loves and hopes till the last, for you were always in them. *Fruit-Gathering.*

God honours me when I work,
He loves me when I sing. *Fireflies.*

February 11

Life is given to us, we earn it by giving it. *Stray Birds.*

Love gives freedom while it binds, for love is what unites. *Thought Relics.*

Each rose that comes brings me greetings from the Rose of an eternal spring. *Fireflies.*

FEBRUARY 12

FEBRUARY 13

FEBRUARY 14

February 12

Blessed is he whose fame does not outshine his truth.
Stray Birds.

In love we find a joy which is ultimate because it is the ultimate truth. *Creative Unity.*

In your dark eyes the coming of the rain finds its music.
Lover's Gift.

February 13

Let your life dance lightly on the edges of time, like dew on the tip of a leaf. *Gardener.*

I have a letter from my Beloved: in this letter is an unutterable message, and now my fear of death is done away. *Kabir's Poems.*

Your laughter is like the moonlight breaking through the window of your lips, when the moon is hiding in your heart. *Lover's Gift.*

February 14

As I gaze on your face, mystery overwhelms me: you who belong to all have become mine. *Crescent Moon.*

When I hold the lamp of love in my heart, its light falls on you, and I am left standing behind in the shadow.
Fruit-Gathering.

The darkness of night is in harmony with day,
The morning of mist is discordant. *Fireflies.*

FEBRUARY 15

FEBRUARY 16

FEBRUARY 17

February 15

We come nearest to the great when we are great in humility. *Stray Birds.*

Many a song I had sung to you, morning and evening, and the last one you carried in your voice as you went away. *Lover's Gift.*

This song of mine will wind its music around you like the fond arms of love. *Crescent Moon.*

February 16

The sweetness of thy name fills my heart, when I forget mine—like the morning sun when the mist is melted. *Stray Birds.*

Now that youth has ebbed, I can hear the music of all things, and the sky opens to me its heart of stars. *Lover's Gift.*

The world, in its own true aspect, is full of beauty and joy. *Reminiscences.*

February 17

The silent night has the beauty of the mother, and the clamorous day of the child. *Stray Birds.*

He has seen under new veils the face of the one beloved. *Lover's Gift.*

Migratory songs wing from my heart and seek their nests in your voice of love. *Fireflies.*

February 18

February 19

February 20

February 18

In far distant days, summer will come to the lovers' garden. *Fugitive.*

I long to sit silent by you. But I dare not, lest my heart come out at my lips. *Gardener.*

At sunrise, open and raise your heart like a blossoming flower:

And at sunset, bend your head and in silence complete the worship of the day. *Crescent Moon.*

February 19

Let me sit in peace and listen to thy words in the soul of thy silence. *Crossing.*

The morning light has flooded my eyes—this is thy message to my heart. *Gitanjali.*

The sea of danger, doubt and denial, around man's little island of certainty, challenges him to dare the unknown. *Fireflies.*

February 20

Let all my songs gather together into a single current and flow to a sea of silence in one salutation to thee.

Gitanjali.

Spread this little moment wide across thy lap, holding it under thy light. *Crossing.*

On the seashore of endless worlds is the great meeting of children. *Crescent Moon.*

February 21

February 22

February 23

February 21

The flute of the infinite is played without ceasing, and its sound is love. *Kabir's Poems.*

Humanity for ages has been busy with the one creation of spiritual life. *Creative Unity.*

I have given my heart in secret love to him. I am waiting with my all in the hope of losing everything. *King of Dark Chamber.*

February 22

Wrong cannot afford defeat, but Right can. *Stray Birds.*

Look, my Queen, there on the eastern horizon comes the dawn. *King of Dark Chamber.*

I ask for no reward for the songs I sang you :
I shall be content if they live through the night. *Fugitive.*

February 23

God waits for man to regain his childhood in wisdom. *Stray Birds.*

The child cries out when from the right breast the mother takes it away, in the very next moment to find in the left one its consolation. *Gitanjali.*

She had reached a region where dreams and reality had clasped their hands in friendship. *Broken Ties.*

February 24

February 25

February 26

February 24

The Dweller within can only come to me along my own true path. *Broken Ties.*

Faith is a spiritual organ of sight which enables us instinctively to realise the vision of wholeness when in fact we only see the parts. *Thought Relics.*

Let all my mind bend down at thy door in one salutation to thee. *Gitanjali.*

February 25

Chastity is a wealth that comes from abundance of love. *Stray Birds.*

I am poured forth in living notes of joy and sorrow by your breath. *Creative Unity.*

Strengthen me on errands of danger. *Fugitive.*

February 26

God's silence ripens man's thoughts into speech.
Stray Birds.

You shall meet me again and again in your voyage of life from shore to shore.
Lover's Gift.

Beauty is truth's smile when she beholds her own face in a perfect mirror. *Fireflies.*

February 27

February 28

February 29

FEBRUARY 27

God grows weary of great kingdoms, but never of little flowers. *Stray Birds.*

Honour me with pain. *Fugitive.*

I dive down into the depth of the ocean of forms hoping to gain the perfect pearl of the formless. *Gitanjali.*

FEBRUARY 28

Let me feel this world as thy love taking form, then my love will help it. *Stray Birds.*

Thou art the sky and thou art the nest as well. *Gitanjali.*

Pride engraves his frowns in stones,
Love offers her surrender in flowers. *Fireflies.*

FEBRUARY 29

Every child comes with the message that God is not yet discouraged of man. *Stray Birds.*

You are no longer before my songs, but one with them. *Lover's Gift.*

Do not keep your secret to yourself, my love, but whisper it gently to me, only to me. *Reminiscences.*

MARCH

I HAVE met thee, where the night touches the edge of the day;

Where the light startles the darkness into dawn,
And the waves carry the kiss of one shore to the other.

From the heart of the fathomless blue comes one golden call,
And across the dusk of tears I try to gaze at thy face
And know not for certain if thou art seen.

Crossing.

March 1

March 2

March 1

The sky pours its light into our hearts.

Cycle of Spring.

We hasten to gather our flowers lest they are plundered by the passing winds. *Gardener.*

The hill in its longing for the far-away sky wishes to be like the cloud with its endless urge of seeking.

Fireflies.

March 2

God kisses the finite in his love and man the infinite.

Stray Birds.

The whole universe is assisting this desire that I should be. *Thought Relics.*

Love is an endless mystery, for it has nothing else to explain it. *Fireflies.*

March 3

March 4

March 5

March 3

Let not my life be torn to tatters by penury of waste.
Crossing.

A father's love, like God's rain, does not judge but is poured forth from an abounding source. *Fugitive.*

God in his temple of stars, waits for man to bring him his lamp. *Fireflies.*

March 4

That love can ever lose is a fact that we cannot accept as truth. *Stray Birds.*

It is sweet to sit in a corner and muse and write rhymes that you are all my world. *Gardener.*

The southern gate is unbarred. Come, my Spring, come. Come in the lisping leaves, in the youthful surrender of flowers. *King of Dark Chamber.*

March 5

He who wants to do good knocks at the gate; he who loves finds the gate open. *Stray Birds.*

My Master's flute sounds through all things.
Fugitive.

Love remains a secret even when spoken, for only a lover truly knows that he is loved. *Fireflies.*

March 6

March 7

March 8

March 6

'How far are you from me, O Fruit?'
'I am hidden in your heart, O Flower.'

Stray Birds.

Open your eyes and see. Feel this world as a living flute might feel the breath of music passing through it.

Thought Relics.

We cannot see Beauty till we let go our hold of it.

Home and the World.

March 7

God comes to me in the dusk of my evening with the flowers from my past kept fresh in his basket.

Stray Birds.

Mirth spreads from leaf to leaf, my darling, and gladness without measure. The heaven's river has drowned its banks and the flood of joy is abroad. *Gitanjali.*

My work is rewarded in daily wages.
I wait for my final value in love. *Fireflies.*

March 8

'You are the big drop of dew under the lotus leaf, I am the smaller one on its upper side,' said the dewdrop to the lake. *Stray Birds.*

The quest of the unattained is the great impulse in man which brings forth all his best creations.

Thought Relics.

Great is the festival hall where you are to be the only guest:
Therefore the letter to you is written from sky to sky.

Creative Unity.

March 9

March 10

March 11

March 9

The noise of the moment scoffs at the music of the Eternal. *Stray Birds.*

Thou givest thyself to me in love, and then feelest thine own entire sweetness in me. *Gitanjali.*

I am able to love my God, because he gives me freedom to deny him. *Fireflies.*

March 10

When all the strings of my life are tuned, my Master, then at every touch of thine will come out the music of love. *Stray Birds.*

God is freedom, for he is light. *Thought Relics.*

I will pour my songs into your mute heart, and my love into your love. *Gardener.*

March 11

Bring him not into your house as the guest of your eyes ; but let him come at your heart's invitation. *Creative Unity.*

It is the same life that is rocked in the ocean cradle of birth and of death, in ebb and in flow. *Gitanjali.*

'I love, I love,' is the cry that breaks out from the bosom of earth and water. *Red Oleanders.*

March 12

March 13

March 14

March 12

Be still, my heart, these great trees are prayers.
Stray Birds.

No, it is not yours to open buds into blossoms. Shake the bud, strike it, it is beyond your power to make it blossom. *Fruit-Gathering.*

The shade of my tree is for passers-by, its fruit for the one for whom I wait. *Fireflies.*

March 13

If love be denied me, then why does the morning break its heart in songs? *Crossing.*

The light that fills the sky seeks its limit in a dewdrop on the grass. *Fireflies.*

Day by day thou art making me worthy of thy simple great gifts. *Gitanjali.*

March 14

I have been travelling to seek you, my friend, for long.
Creative Unity.

Bring beauty and order into my forlorn life.
Lover's Gift.

When the hour strikes for thy silent worship, command me, my Master, to sing. *Gitanjali.*

March 15

March 16

March 17

March 15

Make way, O bud, make way. Burst open thy heart and make way. *Creative Unity.*

The sky remains infinitely vacant for earth there to build its heaven with dreams. *Fireflies.*

When in the morning air the golden harp is tuned, honour me, my master, commanding my presence. *Gitanjali.*

March 16

Every step I take is in my Master's house. *Fugitive.*

There was a time when my life was like a bud. All its perfume was stored in its core. *Gardener.*

The human heart is a vast wilderness, whose interlacing forest branches rock darkness like an infant. *Reminiscences.*

March 17

The prelude of the night is commenced in the music of the sunset, in its solemn hymn to the ineffable dark. *Stray Birds.*

Love counts no cost too great to realise its truth. *Thought Relics.*

In this morning light I do not know what it is that my heart desires. *Reminiscences.*

March 18

March 19

March 20

March 18

If to leave this world be as real as to love it—then there must be a meaning in the meeting and parting of life.
Fruit-Gathering.

Its store of snow is the hill's own burden, its outpouring of streams is borne by all the world. *Fireflies.*

Where shall I meet him, the Man of my Heart?
He is lost to me and I seek him wandering from land to land. *Creative Unity.*

March 19

If you shut your door to all errors truth will be shut out. *Stray Birds.*

Heaven is fulfilled in your sweet body, my child.
Lover's Gift.

As the tree its leaves, I shed my words on the earth; let my thoughts unuttered flower in thy silence.
Fireflies.

March 20

Whatever I have to leave, let me leave; and whatever I have to bear, let me bear. Only, let me walk with thee.
Creative Unity.

Let your love see me even through the barrier of nearness. *Fireflies.*

There was a tiny flower among thorns and I cried, 'The world's hope is not dead'. *Fugitive.*

March 21

March 22

March 23

March 21

Our names are the light that glows on the sea-waves at night and then dies without leaving its signature.

Stray Birds.

Oh, grant me my prayer that I may never lose the bliss of the touch of the One in the play of the many.

Gitanjali.

The spirit of work in creation is there to carry and help the spirit of play. *Fireflies.*

March 22

'In the moon thou sendest thy love-letters to me,' said the night to the sun.

'I leave my answers in tears upon the grass.'

Stray Birds.

The light is shattered into gold on every cloud, my darling, and it scatters gems in profusion. *Gitanjali.*

My faith in truth, my vision of the perfect, help thee, Master, in thy creation. *Fireflies.*

March 23

Leisure in its activity is work.
The stillness of the sea stirs in waves. *Stray Birds.*

Faith is the bird that feels the light and sings when the dawn is still dark. *Fireflies.*

The fountain of life splashes and foams in laughter and tears. *Reminiscences.*

March 24

March 25

March 26

March 24

Let him only see the thorns who has eyes to see the rose. *Stray Birds.*

We cannot truly live for one another if we never claim the freedom to live alone. *Thought Relics.*

Let my love find its strength in the service of day, its peace in the union of night. *Fireflies.*

March 25

The leaf becomes flower when it loves.
The flower becomes fruit when it worships.
Stray Birds.

At every footfall of yours, will not the harp of the road break out in sweet music of pain? *Gitanjali.*

Let me go about in your kingdom accepting your call. *Crossing.*

March 26

The roots below the earth claim no reward for making the branches fruitful. *Stray Birds.*

Come, moon, come down, kiss my darling on the forehead. *Lover's Gift.*

All the delights that I have felt in life's fruits and flowers, let me offer to thee at the end of the feast in a perfect union of love. *Fireflies.*

March 27

March 28

March 29

March 27

Man's revelation does not lie in the fact that he is a power, but that he is a spirit. *Creative Unity.*

What divine drink wouldst thou have, my God, from this overflowing cup of my life? *Gitanjali.*

You have floated down the stream of the world's life, and at last you have stranded on my heart.
Crescent Moon.

March 28

Creation is the harmony of contrary forces—the forces of attraction and repulsion. *Creative Unity.*

Religion, like poetry, is not a mere idea, it is expression.
Thought Relics.

I have had my invitation to this world's festival, and thus my life has been blessed. *Gitanjali.*

March 29

With a glance of your eyes, you could plunder all the wealth of songs struck from poets' harps. *Gardener.*

O friend, thy body is God's lyre; he tightens its strings and draws forth from it his own melody.
Kabir's Poems.

The tree is a winged spirit released from the bondage of seed pursuing its adventure of life across the unknown.
Fireflies.

March 30

March 31

March 30

This life is the crossing of a sea, where we meet in the same narrow ship. *Stray Birds.*

God eludes us in nature to call us onward; in the soul he surrenders himself to gather us to his heart.

Thought Relics.

I know that this is nothing but thy love, O beloved of my heart—this golden light that dances upon the leaves.

Gitanjali.

March 31

It was my part at this world's festival to play upon my instrument, my master,

And I have done all I could. *Gitanjali.*

In the realm of power we grow by aggrandisement; but in the realm of love we grow by renunciation.

Thought Relics.

My heart is full as I look around me and see the silent sky and the flowing water, and feel that happiness is spread abroad as simply as a smile on a child's face.

Lover's Gift.

SPRING

COME, Spring, reckless lover of the earth, make the forest's heart pant for utterance.

Come in gusts of disquiet where the flowers break open and jostle the new leaves.

Burst like a rebellion of light, through the night's vigil, through the lake's dark dumbness, through the dungeon under the dust, proclaiming freedom to the shackled seeds.

Like the laughter of lightning, like the shout of a storm, break into the midst of the noisy town ; free stifled word and unconscious effort, reinforce our flagging fight and conquer death.

Fugitive.

RABINDRANATH TAGORE IN 1877

APRIL

G

HAVE you not heard his silent steps. He comes, comes, ever comes.

Every moment and every age, every day and every night, he comes, comes, ever comes.

Many a song have I sung in many a mood of mind, but all their notes have always proclaimed, ' He comes, comes, ever comes '.

In the fragrant days of sunny April through the forest path he comes, comes, ever comes.

In the rainy gloom of July nights on the thundering chariot of clouds, he comes, comes, ever comes.

In sorrow after sorrow it is his steps that press upon my heart, and it is the golden touch of his feet that makes my joy to shine.

Gitanjali.

APRIL 1

APRIL 2

April 1

The sunlight opens for me the world's gate, love's light its treasure. *Fireflies.*

One final glance from thine eyes and my life will be ever thine own. *Gitanjali.*

The hills are like shouts of children who raise their arms trying to catch stars. *Stray Birds.*

April 2

Art is the expression of the universal through the individual. *Thought Relics.*

I carry in my world that flourishes the worlds that have failed. *Stray Birds.*

My life, like the reed with its stops, has its play of colours through the gaps in its hopes and gains. *Fireflies.*

April 3

April 4

April 5

April 3

Men are cruel, but Man is kind. *Stray Birds.*

God loves to see in me, not his servant, but himself who serves all. *Fireflies.*

I know the touch of her blown hair in all my dreams. *Lover's Gift.*

April 4

Consciousness is the light by the help of which we travel along our path of life. *Thought Relics.*

There are seekers of wisdom and seekers of wealth.
I seek thy company so that I may sing. *Fireflies.*

God waits to win back his own flowers as gifts from man's hands. *Stray Birds.*

April 5

All my illusions will burn into illumination of joy, and all my desires ripen into fruits of love. *Gitanjali.*

Man's world is the history of his aspirations interrupted and renewed. *Creative Unity.*

Let me not bend my heart to the yoke of the many. *Crossing.*

April 6

April 7

April 8

April 6

Truth is over all, and beauty is the expression of truth.
Thought Relics.

Between the shores of Me and Thee there is the loud ocean, my own surging self, which I long to cross.
Fireflies.

My poet, is it thy delight to see thy creation through my eyes? *Gitanjali.*

April 7

The sky pours its light into our hearts.
Cycle of Spring.

I know that the magic of your face is not all its own, but has stolen the passionate light that was in my eyes at some immemorial meeting. *Fugitive.*

Spiritual life is the emancipation of consciousness.
Thought Relics.

April 8

There comes the morning with the golden basket in her right hand bearing the wreath of beauty, silently to crown the earth. *Gitanjali.*

When we are more to ourselves, then the world is less to us. *Thought Relics.*

The night opens the flowers in secret and allows the day to get thanks. *Stray Birds.*

April 9

April 10

April 11

April 9

Truth loves its limits, for there it meets the beautiful. *Fireflies.*

God's great power is in the gentle breeze, not in the storm. *Stray Birds.*

The sun breaks out from the clouds on the day when I must go, and the sky gazes upon the earth like God's wonder. *Crossing.*

April 10

Rest belongs to the work as the eyelids to the eyes. *Stray Birds.*

Existence is the play of the fountain of immortality. *Thought Relics.*

My poet, is it thy delight to stand at the portal of my ears, silently to listen to thine own eternal harmony? *Gitanjali.*

April 11

My heart is sad, for it knows not from where comes its call. *Crossing.*

Thought feeds itself with its own words and grows. *Stray Birds.*

Could the child bring such a joy to the heart of man if age and death were true? *Thought Relics.*

April 12

April 13

April 14

April 12

I see thy silent figure and suddenly catch thine eyes gazing upon me. *Crossing.*

The speech of my heart will be carried on in murmurings of a song. *Gitanjali.*

My offerings are not for the temple at the end of the road, but for the wayside shrines that surprise me at every bend. *Fireflies.*

April 13

That which oppresses me, is it my soul trying to come out in the open, or the soul of the world knocking at my heart for its entrance? *Stray Birds.*

Wisdom has the character of the child perfected through knowledge and feeling. *Thought Relics.*

The joy ran from all the world to build my body. *Fruit-Gathering.*

April 14

I feel that all the stars shine in me. The world breaks into my life like a flood. *Fruit-Gathering.*

Steersman, sit at the helm, for my boat is fretting to be free. *Crossing.*

She who ever has remained in the depth of my being, in the twilight of gleams. *Gitanjali.*

April 15

April 16

April 17

April 15

The water in a vessel is sparkling; the water in the sea is dark.

The small truth has words that are clear; the great truth has great silence. *Stray Birds.*

By extinguishing the fire of pain man may find his comfort; but by mastering this fire, he lights his lamp of wisdom. *Thought Relics.*

The morning light has flooded my eyes—this is thy message to my heart. *Gitanjali.*

April 16

It is the little things that I leave behind for my loved ones,—great things are for everyone. *Stray Birds.*

From the words of the poet men take what meanings please them; yet their last meaning points to Thee. *Gitanjali.*

My clouds, sorrowing in the dark, forget that they themselves have hidden the sun. *Fireflies.*

April 17

Woman, thou hast encircled the world's heart with the depth of thy tears as the sea has the earth. *Stray Birds.*

The eternal repeats its call at man's gate in every child, and the morning's message keeps its melody unimpaired. *Thought Relics.*

True end is not in the reaching of the limit, but in a completion which is limitless. *Fireflies.*

APRIL 18

APRIL 19

APRIL 20

April 18

Rare is the world's lowliest seat, rare is its meanest of lives. *Gitanjali.*

The tree gazes in love at its own beautiful shadow which yet it never can grasp. *Fireflies.*

Life's opportunity is to be able to offer hospitality to our God. *Thought Relics.*

April 19

Woman, in your laughter you have the music of the fountain of life. *Stray Birds.*

Man knows himself as great where he sees great men. *Thought Relics.*

Let my love like sunlight surround you and yet give you illumined freedom. *Fireflies.*

April 20

God loves man's lamp-lights better than his own great stars. *Stray Birds.*

All that I am, that I have, that I hope and all my love have ever flowed towards thee in depth of secrecy. *Gitanjali.*

My offerings are too timid to claim your remembrance, and therefore you may remember them. *Fireflies.*

APRIL 21

APRIL 22

APRIL 23

April 21

'I have lost my dewdrop,' cries the flower to the morning sky that has lost all its stars. *Stray Birds.*

I have found my place in the feast of thy songs in April. *Crossing.*

There were moments when you sang your songs to me; and as my pride knows, you will remember that I listened and lost my heart. *Fugitive.*

April 22

The best does not come alone.
It comes with the company of the all. *Stray Birds.*

The flower sweetens the air with its perfume; yet its last service is to offer itself to Thee. *Gitanjali.*

Now let me sit in peace and listen to thy words in the soul of my silence. *Crossing.*

April 23

Praise shames me, for I secretly beg for it.
Stray Birds.

Pain finds its own music in the notes that joy brings to it from heaven, as the pebbles find theirs from the flow of the laughing stream. *Thought Relics.*

From the solemn gloom of the temple children run out to sit in the dust,
God watches them play and forgets the priest.
Fireflies.

April 24

April 25

April 26

April 24

The service of the fruit is precious, the service of the flower is sweet, but let my service be the service of the leaves in its shade of humble devotion. *Stray Birds.*

Deliverance is not for me in renunciation. I feel the embrace of freedom in a thousand bonds of delight. *Gitanjali.*

God seeks comrades and claims love. *Fireflies.*

April 25

Life has become richer by the love that has been lost. *Stray Birds.*

The lake lies low by the hill, a tearful entreaty of love at the foot of the inflexible. *Fireflies.*

There, where spreads the infinite sky for the soul to take its flight in, reigns the stainless white radiance. *Gitanjali.*

April 26

Those who have everything but thee, my God, laugh at those who have nothing but thyself. *Stray Birds.*

I have roamed from country to country keeping her in the core of my heart, and around her have risen and fallen the growth and decay of my life. *Gitanjali.*

Let those orphaned days that passed without thee be forgotten. *Crossing.*

April 27

April 28

April 29

April 27

I touch God in my song as the hill touches the far-away sea with its waterfall. *Fireflies.*

Loose the chain and heave the anchor ; we sail by the starlight. *Crossing.*

My heart is sweet with the memory of the first fresh jasmines that filled my hands when I was a child.
Crescent Moon.

April 28

Languor is upon your heart and the slumber is still on your eyes. Has not the word come to you that the flower is reigning in splendour among thorns ?
Wake, oh awaken ! Let not the time pass in vain.
Gitanjali.

Life's play is swift, life's playthings fall behind one by one and are forgotten. *Fireflies.*

I want to give you something, my child, for we are drifting in the stream of the world. *Crescent Moon.*

April 29

Do not say, 'It is morning', and dismiss it with a name of yesterday. See it for the first time as a new-born child that has no name. *Stray Birds.*

It is not the loss of energy, the waning of life, which is peace, but their perfection. *Thought Relics.*

The burden of self is lightened when I laugh at myself.
Fireflies.

April 30

April 30

My songs share their seat in the heart of the world with the music of the clouds and forest. *Gardener.*

Bless this little heart, this white soul; he will follow you, laughing and talking, and not a doubt in his heart.

Clasp him to your heart and bless him.

Crescent Moon.

When the world sleeps I come to your door. The stars are silent and I am afraid to sing. *Fruit-Gathering.*

MAY

WHERE the mind is without fear and the head is held high;

Where knowledge is free;

Where the world has not been broken up into fragments by narrow domestic walls;

Where words come out from the depth of truth;

Where tireless striving stretches its arms towards perfection;

Where the clear stream of reason has not lost its way into the dreary desert sand of dead habit;

Where the mind is led forward by thee into ever-widening thought and action—

Into that heaven of freedom, my Father, let my country awake.

Gitanjali.

May 1

May 2

MAY 1

My holiday must be taken through yours, finding light in the dance of your eyes. *Fugitive.*

It is the fact that we enjoy, which unites us with all things through the relationship of love.

Creative Unity.

As the leaf of the lotus abides on the water,
So Thou art my lord and I am Thy servant.

Kabir's Poems.

MAY 2

The stream of truth flows through its channels of mistakes. *Stray Birds.*

Their number is not small who with their lives sing the epic of the freedom of soul, but will never be known in history. *Thought Relics.*

The fireflies, twinkling among leaves, make the stars wonder. *Fireflies.*

May 3

May 4

May 5

May 3

Thou hast led me through my crowded travels of the day to my evening's loneliness.

I wait for its meaning through the stillness of the night.

Stray Birds.

Who can truly pray for peace? Only they who are ready to renounce. *Thought Relics.*

The mountain remains unmoved at its seeming defeat by the mist. *Fireflies.*

May 4

Lord, I have come to thee, to be taken into the path of the Supreme Truth. *Fruit-Gathering.*

While the rose said to the sun, 'I shall ever remember thee', her petals fell to the dust. *Fireflies.*

Accept me, Lord, accept me for this while.

Do not turn away thy face from my heart's dark secrets. *Crossing.*

May 5

'How may I sing to thee and worship thee, O Sun?' asked the little flower.

'By the simple silence of thy purity,' answered the sun. *Stray Birds.*

Men of tranquil mind never seek the eternal in things of the moment. *Thought Relics.*

The dewdrop knows the sun only within its own tiny orb. *Fireflies.*

May 6

May 7

May 8

May 6

The wind is stirred into the murmur of music at this time of my departure. *Crossing.*

The world speaks to me in pictures, my soul answers in music. *Fireflies.*

Thus it is that thy joy in me is so full.

O, thou lord of the heavens, where would be thy love if I were not? *Gitanjali.*

May 7

We live in this world when we love it. *Stray Birds.*

In life's growth every stage has its perfection, the flower as well as the fruit. *Thought Relics.*

The sky tells its beads all night on the countless stars in memory of the sun. *Fireflies.*

May 8

Let the dead have the immortality of fame, but the living the immortality of love. *Stray Birds.*

It is the function of our soul to build its heaven upon the foundation of the earth. *Thought Relics.*

The darkness of night, like pain, is dumb; the darkness of dawn, like peace, is silent. *Fireflies.*

May 9

May 10

May 11

May 9

Ever in my life have I sought thee with my songs.
Gitanjali.

Some have thought deeply and explored the meaning of thy truth, and they are great;
I have listened to catch the music of thy play, and I am glad. *Fireflies.*

Let me not pursue many paths to gather many things.
Crossing.

May 10

The dim silence of my mind seems filled with crickets' chirp—the grey twilight of sound. *Stray Birds.*

It was my songs that taught me all the lessons I ever learnt. *Gitanjali.*

The lotus offers its beauty to the heaven, the grass its service to the earth. *Fireflies.*

May 11

My heart is homesick to-day for the one sweet hour across the sea of time. *Stray Birds.*

That we have been wounded is a fact which can be ignored, but that we have been brave is a truth of the highest importance. *Thought Relics.*

The night is dark, my Lord, and thy pilgrim is blinded. Hold thou my hand. *Crossing.*

MAY 12

MAY 13

MAY 14

May 12

The bird-song is the echo of the morning light back from the earth. *Stray Birds.*

Deliver me from my own shadows, my Lord, from the wrecks and confusion of my days. *Crossing.*

O thou beautiful, there in the nest it is thy love that encloses the soul. *Gitanjali.*

May 13

Let only that little be left of me whereby I may never hide thee. *Gitanjali.*

It is in our own consciousness that the universe knows itself. *Thought Relics.*

Thou hast given me thy love, filling the world with thy gifts. *Crossing.*

May 14

Dark clouds become heaven's flowers when kissed by light. *Stray Birds.*

If but once you should raise your loving eyes to my face, it would make my life sweet beyond death. *Gardener.*

Through the silent night I hear the returning vagrant hopes of the morning knock at my heart. *Fireflies.*

MAY 15

MAY 16

MAY 17

May 15

The night's silence, like a deep lamp, is burning with the light of its milky way. *Stray Birds.*

What comes from your willing hands I take. I beg for nothing more. *Gardener.*

My new love comes, bringing to me the eternal wealth of the old. *Fireflies.*

May 16

Is not this mountain like a flower, with its petals of hills, drinking the sunlight? *Stray Birds.*

Grant me that I may not be a coward, feeling your mercy in my success alone; but let me find the grasp of your hand in my failure. *Fruit Gathering.*

When the shroud of darkness will be lifted from my soul, it will bring music to thy smile. *Crossing.*

May 17

Find your beauty, my heart, from the world's movement, like the boat that has the grace of the wind and the water. *Stray Birds.*

On the seashore of endless worlds is the great meeting of children. *Gitanjali.*

When thou savest me, my Lord, the steps are lighter in the march of thy worlds. *Crossing.*

May 18

May 19

May 20

May 18

We fulfil our destiny when we go back from forms to joy, from law to love, when we untie the knot of the finite and hark back to the infinite. *Sadhana.*

Trust love even if it brings sorrow. Do not close up your heart. *Gardener.*

My mind has its true union with thee, O sky, at the window which is mine own, and not in the open where thou hast thy sole kingdom. *Fireflies.*

May 19

My holiday is an endless freedom for love to disturb me. *Fugitive.*

Love is the perfection of consciousness. *Sadhana.*

When we know the Infinite Soul as the final truth, then through our union with it we realise the joy of our soul. *Creative Unity.*

May 20

My life's empty flute waits for its final music like the primal darkness before the stars came out. *Fireflies.*

We never can have a true view of man unless we have a love for him. *Sadhana.*

Our consciousness of this world is perfect when it realises all things as spiritually one with itself.
Creative Unity.

May 21

May 22

May 23

May 21

Lift me into thy world and let me have the freedom gladly to lose my all. *Stray Birds.*

Make way, O bud, make way, burst open thy heart and make way. The opening spirit has overtaken thee, canst thou remain a bud any longer? *Fugitive.*

Emancipation from the bondage of the soil is no freedom for the tree. *Fireflies.*

May 22

My heart, with its lapping waves of song, longs to caress this green world of the sunny day. *Stray Birds.*

All is done and finished in the eternal heaven. But earth's flowers of illusion are kept eternally fresh by death. *Gardener.*

The tapestry of life's story is woven with the threads of life's ties ever joining and breaking. *Fireflies.*

May 23

Wayside grass, love the star, then your dreams will come out in flowers. *Stray Birds.*

He who can open the bud does it so simply. He gives it a glance, and the life-sap stirs through its veins. *Fruit-Gathering.*

My heart sits in the shadow of the rains, waiting for thy love. *Crossing.*

May 24

May 25

May 26

May 24

Is reaching the shore a greater prize than losing myself with you? *Fugitive.*

My soul to-night loses itself in the silent heart of a tree standing alone among the whispers of immensity. *Fireflies.*

Hold thy faith firm, my heart,
The day will dawn. *Crossing.*

May 25

Knowledge is precious to us, because we shall never have time to complete it. *Gardener.*

Let not my thanks to thee rob my silence of its fuller homage. *Fireflies.*

The light of thy music illumines the world.
The life breath of thy music runs from sky to sky. *Gitanjali.*

May 26

I have sung the songs of thy day.
In the evening let me carry thy lamp through the stormy path. *Stray Birds.*

The same stream of life that runs through my veins night and day runs through the world and dances in rhythmic measures. *Gitanjali.*

Life's aspirations come in the guise of children. *Fireflies.*

May 27

May 28

May 29

May 27

I do not ask thee into the house.
Come into my infinite loneliness, my Lover.
Stray Birds.

Love unexpressed is sacred; it shines like gems in the gloom of the hidden heart. *Gardener.*

The faded flower sighs that the spring has vanished for ever. *Fireflies.*

May 28

The trembling leaves of this tree touch my heart like the fingers of an infant child. *Stray Birds.*

Children have their play on the seashore of worlds.
Gitanjali.

In my life's garden my wealth has been of the shadows and lights that are never gathered and stored. *Fireflies.*

May 29

Let your music, like a sword, pierce the noise of the market to its heart. *Stray Birds.*

Let me not crave in anxious fear to be saved, but hope for the patience to win my freedom. *Fruit-Gathering.*

The fruit that I have gained for ever is that which thou hast accepted. *Fireflies.*

May 30

May 31

May 30

I have learnt the simple meaning of thy whispers in flowers and sunshine. *Stray Birds.*

The great power of beauty is in its modesty. It must have our all or nothing, therefore it never asks. *Thought Relics.*

The jasmine knows the sun to be her brother in the heaven. *Fireflies.*

May 31

Let me not look for allies in life's battlefield, but to my own strength. *Fruit-Gathering.*

The wistful face of the earth, weaving its autumn mists, wakens longing in my heart. *Crossing.*

Over my thoughts and actions, my slumbers and dreams, she reigned yet dwelled alone and apart. *Gitanjali.*

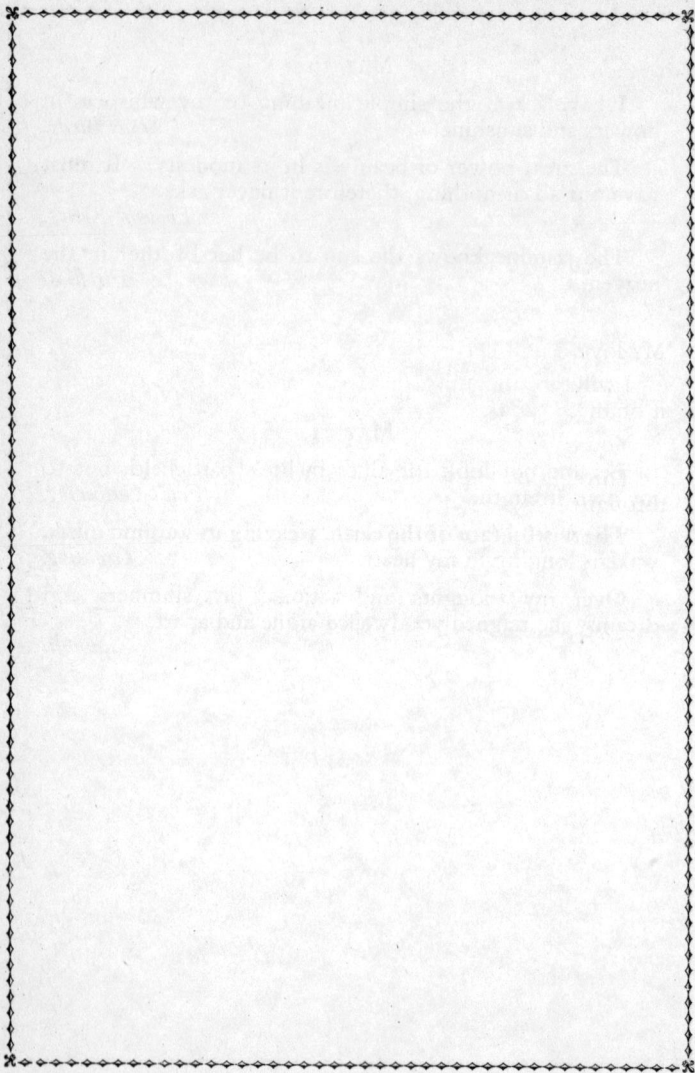

SUMMER

My love, I will keep you hidden in my eyes:

I will thread your image like a gem on my joy and hang it on my bosom.

You have been in my heart ever since I was a child,

Throughout my youth, throughout my life, even through all my dreams.

You dwell in my being when I sleep and when I wake.

Fugitive.

JUNE

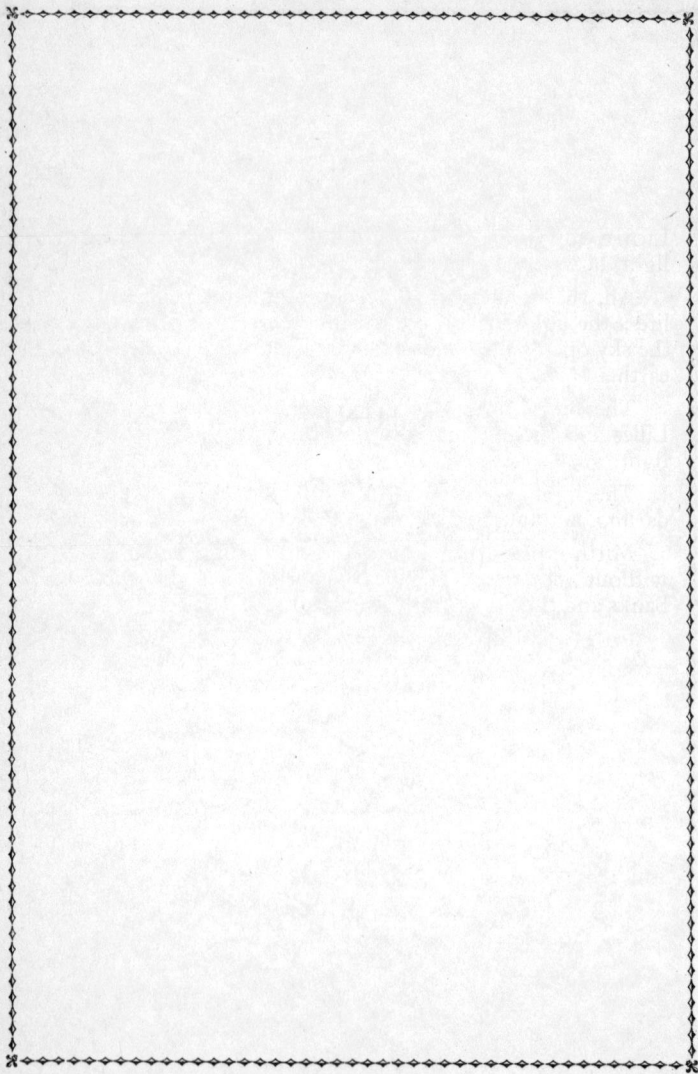

Light, my light, the world-filling light, the eye-kissing light, heart-sweetening light!

Ah, the light dances, my darling, at the centre of my life; the light strikes, my darling, the chords of my love; the sky opens, the wind runs wild, laughter passes over the earth.

The butterflies spread their sails on the sea of light. Lilies and jasmines surge up on the crest of the waves of light.

The light is shattered into gold on every cloud, my darling, and it scatters gems in profusion.

Mirth spreads from leaf to leaf, my darling, and gladness without measure. The heaven's river has drowned its banks and the flood of joy is abroad.

Gitanjali.

JUNE 1

JUNE 2

June 1

Let my thoughts come to you, when I am gone, like the afterglow of sunset at the margin of starry silence.
Stray Birds.

The true meaning of living is outliving, it is ever growing out of itself. *Thought Relics.*

Behind the silent dark walks the Unseen Comer, and my heart trembles. *Crossing.*

June 2

Light in my heart the evening star of rest, and then let the night whisper to me of love. *Stray Birds.*

Let me not beg for the stilling of my pain, but for the heart to conquer it. *Fruit-Gathering.*

The Hidden Banner is planted in the temple of the sky :
Still your mind to silence before that splendour.
Kabir's Poems.

June 3

June 4

June 5

June 3

The day of work is done. Hide my face in your arms, Mother.

Let me dream. *Stray Birds.*

We must pay our homage to God where he rules ; but we may laugh at him where he loves. *Thought Relics.*

Your voice, free bird, reaches my sleeping nest, and my drowsy wings dream of a voyage to the light above the clouds. *Fireflies.*

June 4

Let me not pray to be sheltered from dangers, but to be fearless in facing them. *Fruit-Gathering.*

You came to my door in the dawn and sang. *Crossing.*

I see with eyes open and smile, and behold his beauty everywhere. *Kabir's Poems.*

June 5

I have seen thee as the half-awakened child sees his mother in the dusk of the dawn and then smiles and sleeps again. *Stray Birds.*

Music fills the infinite between two souls. *Fugitive.*

I have stilled my restless mind, and my heart is radiant. *Kabir's Poems.*

June 6

June 7

June 8

June 6

While I was passing with the crowd in the road I saw thy smile from the balcony, and I sang and forgot all noise.
Stray Birds.

Our will attains its perfection when it is one with love, for only love is true freedom. *Thought Relics.*

When I awake in thy love, my night of ease will be ended.
The sunrise will touch my heart with its touchstone of fire. *Crossing.*

June 7

There is an anguish in my heart for the burden of its riches not given to you. *Fruit-Gathering.*

Dead leaves when they lose themselves in soil take part in the life of the forest. *Fireflies.*

Where the mind is without fear and the head is held high. *Gitanjali.*

June 8

Love's pain sang round my life like the unplumbed sea, and love's joy sang like birds in its flowering groves.
Stray Birds.

Light, oh, where is the light ? Kindle it with the burning fire of desire. *Gitanjali.*

The mind ever seeks its words from its sounds and silence as the sky from its darkness and light. *Fireflies.*

June 9

June 10

June 11

June 9

Thou art the sky, and thou art the nest as well.

Gitanjali.

Send me the love that keeps the heart still with the fulness of peace. *Fruit-Gathering.*

The unseen dark plays on his flute and the rhythm of light eddies into stars and suns, into thoughts and dreams.

Fireflies.

June 10

They light their own lamps and sing their own words in their temples.

But the birds sing thy name in thine own morning light —for thy name is joy. *Stray Birds.*

How can the body touch the flower which only the spirit may touch ? *Gardener.*

Come to me like summer cloud, spreading thy showers from sky to sky. *Crossing.*

June 11

With every breath we draw we must realise this truth, that we are living in God. *Personality.*

Day offers to the silence of stars his golden lute to be tuned for the endless life. *Fireflies.*

If you remain divided, offering part of yourself to God and part elsewhere, then everything will become difficult.

Gora.

JUNE 12

JUNE 13

JUNE 14

June 12

If thou speakest not, I will fill my heart with thy silence and endure it. *Gitanjali.*

I believe in a spiritual world, not as anything separate from this world, but as its innermost truth. *Personality.*

This world is the world of wild storms kept tame with the music of beauty. *Stray Birds.*

June 13

Who except God visits the poor? *Fugitive.*

The centre is still and silent in the heart of an eternal dance of circles. *Fireflies.*

Thou hast brought the distant near and made a brother of the stranger. *Gitanjali.*

June 14

Sit still, my heart, do not raise your dust.
Let the world find its way to you. *Stray Birds.*

If I call not thee in my prayers, if I keep not thee in my heart, thy love for me still waits for my love. *Gitanjali.*

Spring scatters the petals of flowers that are not for the fruits of the future, but for the moment's whim.
Fireflies.

JUNE 15

JUNE 16

JUNE 17

June 15

The bow whispers to the arrow before it speeds forth—'Your freedom is mine'. *Stray Birds.*

Love spontaneously gives itself in endless gifts. *Sadhana.*

Joy freed from the bonds of earth's slumber rushes into numberless leaves, and dances in the air for a day. *Fireflies.*

June 16

My heart is like the golden casket of thy kiss, said the sunset cloud to the sun. *Stray Birds.*

Love is not a mere sentiment ; it is truth ; it is the joy that is the root of all creation. *Sadhana.*

Woman's smile removes all care from the house : her love is of God's grace. *Sacrifice.*

June 17

By touching you may kill, by keeping away you may possess. *Stray Birds.*

Lay down your flute, my love, leave your arms free to embrace me. *Fugitive.*

My thoughts, like sparks, ride on winged surprises, carrying a single laughter. *Fireflies.*

June 18

June 19

June 20

June 18

The burning log bursts in flame and cries,—'This is my flower, my death'. *Stray Birds.*

Days are coloured bubbles that float upon the surface of fathomless night. *Fireflies.*

I wait for thy shower to come down in the night, when I open my breast and receive it in silence.
Crossing.

June 19

'I cannot keep your waves,' says the bank to the river.
'Let me keep your footprints in my heart.'
Stray Birds.

Give me the supreme courage of love, this is my prayer—the courage to speak, to do, to suffer at thy will, to leave all things or be left alone. *Fugitive.*

The departing night's one kiss on the closed eyes of morning glows in the star of dawn. *Fireflies.*

June 20

The day, with the noise of this little earth, drowns the silence of all worlds. *Stray Birds.*

My mind starts up at some flash on the flow of its thoughts like a brook at a sudden liquid note of its own that is never repeated. *Fireflies.*

I shall make my heart simple and pure and my mind peaceful to be able truly to serve you. *Sacrifice.*

June 21

June 22

June 23

June 21

You came down from your throne and stood at my cottage door. *Gitanjali.*

Teach me thy lessons, O love, give me the power of the weak and the weapon of the unarmed hand. *Chitra.*

Let the last touch of your hands be gentle like the flower of the night. *Gardener.*

June 22

I have met thee where night touches the edge of the day. *Crossing.*

When old words die out on the tongue, new melodies break forth from the heart. *Gitanjali.*

Life is perpetual creation. It has its truth when it outgrows itself in the infinite. *Personality.*

June 23

Maiden, your simplicity, like the blueness of the lake, reveals your depth of truth. *Stray Birds.*

The flute steals the smile from my friend's lips and spreads it over my life. *Fruit-Gathering.*

You are our star, to lead us across the pathless sea of life. *Sacrifice.*

June 24

June 25

June 26

June 24

When the sun goes down to the West, the East of his morning stands before him in silence. *Stray Birds.*

The flower of my desire shall never drop into the dust before it has ripened to fruit. *Chitra.*

The child ever dwells in the mystery of ageless time, unobscured by the dust of history. *Fireflies.*

June 25

Only a portion of my gift is in this world, the rest of it is in my dreams. *Crossing.*

Let love melt into memory and pain into songs. *Gardener.*

A light laughter in the steps of creation carries it swiftly across time. *Fireflies.*

June 26

Night's darkness is a bag that bursts with the gold of the dawn. *Stray Birds.*

If individual notes could claim a prolonged endlessness then they would miss their true eternity which is the music. *Thought Relics.*

I know you will win my heart some day, my lover. *Crossing.*

June 27

June 28

June 29

June 27

Our desire lends the colours of the rainbow to the mere mists and vapours of life. *Stray Birds.*

It is the labour of a lifetime to make one's true self known and honoured. *Chitra.*

Through your stars you gaze deep into my dreams. *Crossing.*

June 28

Someone has secretly left in my hand a flower of love. *Crossing.*

She who is ever returning to God his own outflowing of sweetness, she is the ever-fresh beauty and youth in nature. *Fruit-Gathering.*

There smiles the Divine Child among his playthings of unmeaning clouds and ephemeral lights and shadows. *Fireflies.*

June 29

In love the aim is neither pain nor pleasure but love only. *Fugitive.*

It was only the budding of leaves in the summer, the summer that came into the garden by the sea. *Lover's Gift.*

Thy sunbeam comes upon this earth of mine with outstretched arms. *Gitanjali.*

June 30

June 30

My friend, your great heart shone with the sunrise of the East like the snowy summit of a lonely hill in the dawn.

Stray Birds.

The wisdom of living is in that which gives you the power to give it up. For death is the gate of immortality.

Personality.

The jasmine's lisping of love to the sun is her flowers.

Fireflies.

RABINDRANATH TAGORE AND W. W. PEARSON AT RIVERSIDE, CALIFORNIA

JULY

M

In the deep shadows of the rainy July, with secret steps, thou walkest, silent as night, eluding all watchers.

To-day the morning has closed its eyes, heedless of the insistent calls of the loud east wind, and a thick veil has been drawn over the ever-wakeful blue sky.

The woodlands have hushed their songs and doors are all shut at every house. Thou art the solitary wayfarer in this deserted street.

Oh, my only friend, my best beloved, the gates are all open in my house—do not pass by like a dream.

Gitanjali.

JULY 1

JULY 2

July 1

I think such an evening had come to me only once before in all my births. *Sacrifice.*

Love is lit from love as fire from fire, but whence came the first flame? *Fugitive.*

Perpetual giving up is the truth of life.
The perfection of this is our life's perfection.
Personality.

July 2

The movement of life has its rest in its own music.
Stray Birds.

Leave all thy burdens on his hands who can bear all, and never look behind in regret. *Gitanjali.*

This life of ours has been filled with the gifts of the Divine Giver. *Personality.*

July 3

July 4

July 5

JULY 3

Where man is at his greatest, he is unconscious.
Nationalism.

Light finds her treasure of colours through the antagonism of clouds. *Fireflies.*

The consciousness of the infinite in us proves itself by our joy in giving ourselves out of our abundance.
Personality.

JULY 4

The fact that I am indispensable is proved by the fact that I am. *Thought Relics.*

My heart to-day smiles at its past night of tears like a wet tree glistening in the sun after the rain is over.
Fireflies.

Let us live. Let us have the true joy of life, which is the joy of the poet in pouring himself out in his poems.
Personality.

JULY 5

In heart's perspective the distance looms large.
Stray Birds.

Where the mind is led forward by thee into ever-widening thought and action—into that heaven of freedom, my Father, let my country awake. *Gitanjali.*

I have thanked the trees that have made my life fruitful, but have failed to remember the grass that has ever kept it green. *Fireflies.*

July 6

July 7

July 8

July 6

In many a morning and eve thy footsteps have been heard, and thy messenger has come within my heart and called me in secret. *Gitanjali.*

The one without second is emptiness, the other one makes it true. *Fireflies.*

The most important fact of the present age is that all the different races of man have come together. We have to prove our humanity by solving this problem by the help of our higher nature. *Nationalism.*

July 7

Through the sadness of all things I hear the crooning of the Eternal Mother. *Stray Birds.*

If you cannot love me, beloved, forgive me my pain. Do not look askance at me from afar. I will steal back to my corner and sit in the dark. *Gardener.*

Someone has stolen my heart, and scattered it abroad in the sky. *Crossing.*

July 8

I am a child in the dark.

I stretch my hands through the coverlet of night for thee, Mother. *Stray Birds.*

To wake up in love is not to wake up in a world of sweetness, but in the world of heroic endeavours where life wins its eternity through death, and joy its worth in suffering. *Thought Relics.*

Be not ashamed, my brothers, to stand before the proud and powerful with your white robes of simpleness.

Nationalism.

July 9

July 10

July 11

July 9

Let me not shame thee, Father, who displayest thy glory in thy children. *Stray Birds.*

We have not crushed joy to the utmost to wring from it the wine of pain. *Gardener.*

Have you not heard the tune which the Unstruck Music is playing. *Kabir's Poems.*

July 10

Thy sunshine smiles upon the winter days of my heart, never doubting of its spring flowers. *Stray Birds.*

At the immortal touch of thy hands my little heart loses its limits in joy and gives birth to utterance ineffable. *Gitanjali.*

Let your crown be of humility, your freedom the freedom of the soul. *Nationalism.*

July 11

Thou crossest desert lands of barren years to reach the moment of fulfilment. *Stray Birds.*

Restraint is the gateway of the good. *Thought Relics.*

Build God's throne daily upon the ample bareness of your poverty, and know that what is huge is not great and pride is not everlasting. *Nationalism.*

July 12

July 13

July 14

July 12

Thou wilt find, Eternal Traveller, marks of thy footsteps across my songs. *Stray Birds.*

Come, Peace, thou daughter of God's own great suffering. *Nationalism.*

Beauty is omnipresent, therefore everything is capable of giving us joy. *Sadhana.*

July 13

To-night there is a stir among the palm-leaves, a swell in the sea, Full Moon, like the heart-throb of the world. From what unknown sky hast thou carried in thy silence the aching secret of love? *Stray Birds.*

This is my prayer to thee, my Lord—give me the strength to make my love fruitful in service. *Gitanjali.*

Thy morning waits behind the patient dark of the East, meek and silent. *Nationalism.*

July 14

I dream of a star, an island of light, where I shall be born, and in the depth of its quickening leisure my life will ripen its works. *Stray Birds.*

Whatever is good is true, and can never perish. *Fugitive.*

Darkness is the veiled bride, silently waiting for the errant light to return to her bosom. *Fireflies.*

July 15

July 16

July 17

JULY 15

Joy turns into pain when the door by which it should depart is shut against it. *Chitra.*

The wind of heaven blows, the anchor desperately clutches the mud, and my boat is beating its breast against the chain. *Fireflies.*

He who has seen God and touched him, is freed from all fear and trouble. *Kabir's Poems.*

JULY 16

Man's history is waiting in patience for the triumph of the insulted man. *Stray Birds.*

Bring your offerings of worship for the sacred Sunrise. *Nationalism.*

There is a secret joy in the bosom of the night.
Let me fill my heart with it and carry it in secret all the day. *Crossing.*

JULY 17

Lead me, my Guide, before the light fades, into the valley of quiet where life's harvest mellows into golden wisdom. *Stray Birds.*

Give me the strength to raise my mind high above daily trifles. *Gitanjali.*

My heart bends in worship like a dew-laden flower. *Crossing.*

July 18

July 19

July 20

July 18

I feel thy gaze upon my heart this moment like the sunny silence of the morning upon the lonely field whose harvest is over. *Stray Birds.*

The cloud gives all its gold to the departing sun and greets the rising moon with only a pale smile. *Fireflies.*

There is only one history—the history of Man. All national histories are chapters in the larger one. *Nationalism.*

July 19

Hands cling to hands and eyes linger on eyes: thus begins the record of our hearts. *Gardener.*

Is not this earth also His who made Heaven? *Fruit-Gathering.*

Her wistful face haunts my dreams like the rain at night. *Stray Birds.*

July 20

The music of beauty appeals to our heart with the truth that it is meekness inherits the earth. *Sadhana.*

Reality is the harmony which gives to the component parts of a thing the equilibrium of the whole. *Nationalism.*

The cup of evening overbrimmed with love and music and I sat with someone, the memory of whose face is in that setting star. *Sacrifice.*

July 21

July 22

July 23

July 21

It is the tears of the earth that keep her smiles in bloom. *Stray Birds.*

Give me the strength to surrender my strength to thy will with love. *Gitanjali.*

All evils fly from my heart when I see my Lord. *Kabir's Poems.*

July 22

Some unseen fingers, like an idle breeze, are playing upon my heart the music of the ripples. *Stray Birds.*

I grope for that ultimate You, that bare simplicity of truth. *Chitra.*

He has awaited me for countless ages, for love of me he has lost his heart. *Kabir's Poems.*

July 23

Listen, my heart, to the whispers of the world with which it makes love to you. *Stray Birds.*

Let each separate moment of beauty come to me like a bird of mystery from its unseen nest in the dark bearing a message of music. *Chitra.*

We gain freedom when we have paid the full price for our right to live. *Fireflies.*

July 24

July 25

July 26

July 24

The mystery of creation is like the darkness of night: it is great. *Stray Birds.*

When I woke from my slumber and opened my eyes, I saw thee standing by me, flooding my sleep with thy smile.

How I had feared that the path was long and wearisome and the struggle to reach thee was hard! *Gitanjali.*

Your careless gifts of a moment, like the meteors of an autumn night, catch fire in the depth of my being.

Fireflies.

July 25

You have been in my heart ever since I was a child.

Fugitive.

Let me for ever sit with my hope on the brink of its realisation, and thus end my days. *Chitra.*

Free me, as free as are the birds of the wild, the wanderers of unseen paths. *Crossing.*

July 26

If you have found God, then give yourself utterly, and take him to you. *Kabir's Poems.*

This is the ultimate object of our existence that we must ever know that beauty is truth, truth beauty.

Sadhana.

The highest education is that which makes our life in harmony with all existence. *Personality.*

July 27

July 28

July 29

July 27

These little thoughts are the rustle of leaves; they have their whisper of joy in my mind. *Stray Birds.*

Great peace is in the sky. It seems to gather all the world into its arms. *Sacrifice.*

Pleasure is frail like a dewdrop, while it laughs it dies. But sorrow is strong and abiding.
Let sorrowful love wake in your eyes. *Gardener.*

July 28

This day is dear to me above all other days, for to-day the Beloved Lord is a guest in my house. *Kabir's Poems.*

We have come to this world to accept it, not merely to know it. *Personality.*

My life, like the dewdrop upon a lotus leaf, is trembling upon the heart of this great time. *Sacrifice.*

July 29

When a man does not realise his kinship with the world, he lives in a prison-house whose walls are alien to him. *Sadhana.*

My love of to-day finds no home in the nest deserted by yesterday's love. *Fireflies.*

From the beginning until the ending of time there is love between thee and me. And how shall such love be extinguished? *Kabir's Poems.*

July 30

July 31

July 30

The trees come up to my window like the yearning voice of the dumb earth. *Stray Birds.*

The heart is only for giving away. *Gardener.*

Thou hast vanished from my reach, leaving an impalpable touch in the blue of the sky, an invisible image in the wind moving among the shadows.

Fireflies.

July 31

His own mornings are new surprises to God.

Stray Birds.

The shy shadow in the garden loves the sun in silence. Flowers guess the secret, and smile, while the leaves whisper. *Fireflies.*

Rejoice!
For Night's fetters have broken, the dreams have vanished. *Crossing.*

AUGUST

THOU art the sky and thou art the nest as well.

O thou beautiful, there in the nest it is thy love that encloses the soul with colours and sounds and odours.

There comes the morning with the golden basket in her right hand bearing the wreath of beauty, silently to crown the earth.

And there comes the evening over the lonely meadows deserted by the herds, through trackless paths, carrying cool draughts of peace in her golden pitcher from the western ocean of rest.

But there, where spreads the infinite sky for the soul to take her flight in, reigns the stainless white radiance. There is no day nor night, nor form nor colour, and never, never a word.

Gitanjali.

August 1

August 2

August 1

Essentially man is a lover. His freedom is in love, which is another name for perfect comprehension.

Sadhana.

My faith has come to me perfected in the form of a woman. *Sacrifice.*

Your Lord dwells within you, why need your outward eyes be opened? *Kabir's Poems.*

August 2

The waterfall sings, 'I find my song, when I find my freedom'. *Stray Birds.*

From my heart comes out and dances the image of my own desire.

The gleaming vision flits on. *Gardener.*

I am one with the life of this world. *Sacrifice.*

August 3

August 4

August 5

August 3

Woman, when you move about in your household service your limbs sing like a hill stream among its pebbles. *Stray Birds.*

I came to offer thee a flower, but thou must have all my garden,—
It is thine. *Fireflies.*

I shall make my heart simple and pure, and my mind peaceful. *Sacrifice.*

August 4

The sun goes to cross the Western sea, leaving its last salutation to the East. *Stray Birds.*

Our soul can only find out its truth by unifying itsel with others, and only then it has its joy. *Sadhana.*

Thy word has rent Night's veils: the buds of the morning are opened. *Crossing.*

August 5

Give me the strength never to disown the poor, or bend my knees before insolent might. *Gitanjali.*

Life's greetings spread from the East to the West. *Crossing.*

My untuned strings beg for music in their anguished cry of shame. *Fireflies.*

August 6

August 7

August 8

August 6

The world rushes on over the strings of the lingering heart making the music of sadness. *Stray Birds.*

To understand anything is to find in it something which is our own. *Sadhana.*

The clouded sky to-day bears the vision of the shadow of a divine sadness on the forehead of brooding eternity. *Fireflies.*

August 7

When a man feels the rhythmic throb of the soul-life of the whole world in his own soul, then he is free. *Sadhana.*

Flushed with the glow of sunset earth seems like a ripe fruit ready to be harvested by night. *Fireflies.*

The Supreme is giving himself in his world and I am making it mine, like a poem which I realise by finding myself in it. *Personality.*

August 8

I saw you gathering flowers—clad in white, like the dawn bathed in radiance. And I said, 'Make me proud by allowing me to help you'. *Fugitive.*

Give us strength to love, to love fully, our life in its joys and sorrows, in its gains and losses, in its rise and fall. *Sadhana.*

Child, thou bringest to my heart the babble of the wind and the water, the flowers' speechless secrets, the clouds' dreams, the mute gaze of wonder of the morning sky. *Fireflies.*

August 9

August 10

August 11

August 9

Children are God's own creation. *Personality.*

In love the sense of difference is obliterated and the human soul fulfils its highest purpose in perfection, transcending the limit of itself and reaching across the threshold of the infinite. *Sadhana.*

Put thy cleverness away: love is something other than this, and he who has sought it truly has found it.
Kabir's Poems.

August 10

His blessing would silently flow out to her from the very depth of his heart. *Gora.*

In our pleasures we are confined to ourselves; in the good we are freed and belong to all. *Sadhana.*

Whisper something to my ears, which will overflow this life with sweetness, flooding death itself. *Sacrifice.*

August 11

Like the meeting of the seagulls and the waves we meet and come near.
The seagulls fly off, the waves roll away and we depart.
Stray Birds.

The storm still seeks its end in peace when it strikes against peace with all its might. *Gitanjali.*

My guest has come to my door in the autumn morning.
Sing, my heart, sing thy welcome. *Crossing.*

AUGUST 12

AUGUST 13

AUGUST 14

August 12

My day is done, and I am like a boat drawn on the beach, listening to the dance music of the tide in the evening. *Stray Birds.*

Love is the highest bliss that man can attain, for through it alone he truly knows that he is more than himself, and that he is at one with All. *Sadhana.*

Your Lord is near, yet you are climbing the palm-tree to seek him. *Kabir's Poems.*

August 13

I am thankful that my lot lies with the humble, who suffer. *Fruit-Gathering.*

The revealment of the infinite in the finite is not seen in its perfection in the starry heavens, in the beauty of flowers. It is in the soul of man. *Sadhana.*

Beauty smiles in the confinement of the bud in the heart of a sweet incompleteness. *Fireflies.*

August 14

The perfect decks itself in beauty for the love of the imperfect. *Stray Birds.*

This is my prayer to thee, my lord, strike, strike at the root of penury in my heart. *Gitanjali.*

You did not know yourself when you dwelt alone. *Fruit-Gathering.*

AUGUST 15

AUGUST 16

AUGUST 17

August 15

I came and you awoke and the skies blossomed with light. *Fruit-Gathering.*

Evil has to pass on, it has to grow into good. *Sadhana.*

I have come to thee to take thy touch before I begin the day. *Crossing.*

August 16

He who has seen God—his work and his rest are filled with music: he sheds abroad the radiance of love. *Kabir's Poems.*

In the history of man moments have come when we have heard the music of God's life touching Man's in perfect harmony. *Personality.*

It is our gaze which gives to the blue of the autumn sky its wistful tinge and human yearning. *Reminiscences.*

August 17

The rain falls, and my heart longs for my Lord. Where the rhythm of the world rises and falls thither my heart has reached. *Kabir's Poems.*

Is the song of the sea in tune only with the rising waves? Does it not also sing with the waves that fall? *Fruit-Gathering.*

Listen to the prayer of the forest for its freedom in flowers. *Fireflies.*

AUGUST 18

AUGUST 19

AUGUST 20

August 18

'I give my whole water in joy,' sings the waterfall, 'though little of it is enough for the thirsty.'

Stray Birds.

This autumn has flooded my unburdened mind with an unreasoning joy. *Reminiscences.*

Man is now upon his career of creative life: he is to give from his abundance. *Personality.*

August 19

Where is the fountain that throws up these flowers in a ceaseless outbreak of ecstasy? *Stray Birds.*

.A poet is a true poet when he can make his personal idea joyful to all. *Sadhana.*

I bring to thee, night, my day's empty cup, to be cleaned with thy cool darkness for a new morning's festival.

Fireflies.

August 20

In my solitude of heart I feel the sigh of this widowed evening veiled with mist and rain. *Stray Birds.*

Kindle the lamp of love with thy life. *Gitanjali..*

The mountain fir, in its rustling, modulates the memory of its fights with the storm into a hymn of peace.

Fireflies.

August 21

August 22

August 23

August 21

The mist, like love, plays upon the heart of the hills and brings out surprises of beauty. *Stray Birds.*

If existence were an evil, it would wait for no philosopher to prove it. *Sadhana.*

Let thy love's sunshine kiss the peaks of my thought. *Crossing.*

August 22

I long to dwell in the ever-living life of Man. *Reminiscences.*

Only by discovering the law of life and following it do we become great. *Sadhana.*

In the shady depth of life are the lonely nests of memories that shrink from words. *Fireflies.*

August 23

The poet wind is out over the sea and the forest to seek his own voice. *Stray Birds.*

Let me carry thy love in my life as a harp does its music. *Crossing.*

Life sends up in blades of grass its silent hymn of praise to the unnamed light. *Fireflies.*

AUGUST 24

AUGUST 25

AUGUST 26

August 24

Your voice, my friend, wanders in my heart, like the muffled sound of the sea among those listening pines.
Stray Birds.

Look upon life and death, there is no separation between them; the right hand and the left hand are one and the same. *Kabir's Poems.*

I hold tight thy hand, and thy touch is with me in my loneliness. *Crossing.*

August 25

When Love renounces all limits it reaches Truth.
Kabir's Poems.

The universal power will thwart us where we are small, where we are against the current of things; but it will help us where we are great, where we are in unison with the all. *Sadhana.*

Open thy door to that which must go, for the loss becomes unseemly when obstructed. *Fireflies.*

August 26

Let life be beautiful like summer flowers and death like autumn leaves. *Stray Birds.*

In pain is symbolised the infinite possibility of perfection, the eternal unfolding of joy. *Sadhana.*

Let thy love like stars shine in the darkness of my sleep. *Crossing.*

August 27

August 28

August 29

August 27

Thy gift of the earliest flower came to me this morning. *Crossing.*

Man's will, which is free, must seek for the realisation of its freedom in other wills, which are also free; and in this is the significance of the spiritual life. *Personality.*

Let the touch of thy finger thrill my life's strings and make the music thine and mine. *Fireflies.*

August 28

We gain our freedom when we attain our truest nature. *Sadhana.*

The inner world rounded in my life like a fruit, matured in joy and sorrow, will drop into the darkness of the original soil for some further course of creation. *Fireflies.*

Because the truth of our will is in freedom, therefore all our pure joy is in freedom. *Personality.*

August 29

It came with a message from the land of surprise, and it floated from the verge of sunset with a sigh of sorrow. *Hungry Stones.*

The whole weight of the universe cannot crush out this individuality of mine. *Sadhana.*

Beauty is the harmony realised in things which are bound by law. Love is the harmony in wills which are free. *Personality.*

August 30

August 31

August 30

This longing is for the one who is felt in the dark, but not seen in the day. *Stray Birds.*

In order to be happy we have to submit our individual will to the sovereignty of the universal will. *Sadhana.*

When the voice of the Silent touches my words I know him and therefore I know myself. *Fireflies.*

August 31

It is the function of religion not to destroy our nature but to fulfil it. *Sadhana.*

My last salutations are to them who knew me imperfect and loved me. *Fireflies.*

I will take nothing from others' hands, but will accept all from Him. *Gora.*

SEPTEMBER

DAY after day, O Lord of my life, shall I stand before thee face to face? With folded hands, O Lord of all worlds, shall I stand before thee face to face?

Under thy great sky in solitude and silence, with humble heart shall I stand before thee face to face?

In this laborious world of thine, tumultuous with toil and with struggle, among hurrying crowds shall I stand before thee face to face?

And when my work shall be done in this world, O King of kings, alone and speechless shall I stand before thee face to face?

Gitanjali.

SEPTEMBER 1

SEPTEMBER 2

September 1

The great earth makes herself hospitable with the help of the grass. *Stray Birds.*

When a man loves, giving becomes a matter of joy to him, like the tree's surrender of ripe fruit. *Sadhana.*

Love's gift cannot be given, it waits to be accepted. *Fireflies.*

September 2

Our true freedom is not the freedom from action, but freedom in action. *Sadhana.*

I have lived in love and not in mere time. *Fireflies.*

Deliver me from all that is untrue, and let the True shed pure radiance over my life. *Gora.*

September 3

September 4

September 5

September 3

My King's road that lies still before my house makes my heart wistful. *Crossing.*

Surrender yourself fully to God, accepting him as your only help. *Gora.*

Lucky was my awakening this morning, for I saw my beloved.

The sky was one piece of joy and my life and youth were fulfilled. *Gitanjali.*

September 4

I ask for a moment's indulgence to sit by your side. The works that I have in hand I will finish afterwards. *Gitanjali.*

The beauty of a poem is bound by strict laws, yet it transcends them. *Sadhana.*

He is the only adorable One to me, I have none other. *Kabir's Poems.*

September 5

The sadness of my soul is her bride's veil; it waits to be lifted in the night. *Stray Birds.*

Let my song be simple as the waking in the morning, as the dripping of dew from the leaves. *Crossing.*

Go forward rejoicing, ready with all your strength to choose the Good. *Gora.*

September 6

September 7

September 8

September 6

I think of other ages that floated upon the stream of life and love and death and are forgotten, and I feel the freedom of passing away. *Stray Birds.*

In the very core of the world's heart stands immortal youth. Death and decay cast over its face momentary shadows and pass on. *Sadhana.*

My life when young was like a flower—a flower that loosens a petal or two from her abundance and never feels the loss. *Fruit-Gathering.*

September 7

This old, old day of our earth is born again and again every morning. *Sadhana.*

Is summer's festival only for fresh blossoms and not also for withered leaves and faded flowers?

Fruit-Gathering.

The cloud stood humbly in a corner of the sky.
The morning crowned it with splendour.

Stray Birds.

September 8

Our roots must go deep down into the universal if we would attain the greatness of personality. *Sadhana.*

Few are the wise and the great who sit by my Master, but he has taken the foolish in his arms and made me his servant for ever. *Fruit-Gathering.*

Do not linger to gather flowers to keep them, but walk on, for flowers will keep themselves blooming all your way.

Stray Birds.

SEPTEMBER 9

SEPTEMBER 10

SEPTEMBER 11

September 9

A handful of dust could hide your signal when I did not know its meaning.

Now that I am wiser I read it in all that hid it before.

Fruit-Gathering.

The music of the far-away summer flutters round the Autumn seeking its former nest. *Stray Birds.*

To-day, after the dark night of sorrow, Dawn has come.

Gora.

September 10

Our Self has to gain by its loss and rise by its surrender.

Sadhana.

Be ready to launch forth, my heart! and let those linger who must.

For your name has been called in the morning sky.

Wait for none. *Fruit-Gathering.*

In the creation of the spiritual world we are God's partners. *Personality.*

September 11

Beauty harmonises in itself the limit and the beyond, the law and the liberty. *Sadhana.*

The desire of the bud is for the night and dew, but the blown flower cries for the freedom of light.

Burst your sheath, my heart, and come forth!

Fruit-Gathering.

The touch of the nameless days clings to my heart like moss round the old tree. *Stray Birds.*

September 12

September 13

September 14

September 12

Our life like a river strikes its banks, not to find itself closed in by them, but to realise anew every moment that it has its unending opening towards the sea. *Sadhana.*

I go in search of everlasting youth: I throw away all that is not one with my life, nor as light as my laughter. *Fruit-Gathering.*

In our spiritual attainment, gaining and giving are the same thing. *Personality.*

September 13

Our Self must bend its head low in love and meekness, and take its stand where great and small meet. *Sadhana.*

My wings are full of the desire of the sky. *Fruit-Gathering.*

The early dawn of our union broke through our hearts in overflowing silence. *Sacrifice.*

September 14

To move is to meet you every moment, Fellow-Traveller. *Fruit-Gathering.*

The baby does not know all about its mother's activities, but it knows that she is its mother. *Personality.*

I have my place in your heart, as your beloved, and in your world, as your Queen. *Sacrifice.*

September 15

September 16

September 17

September 15

Outwardly nature is busy and restless, inwardly she is all silence and peace. *Sadhana.*

He who throws his doors open and steps onward receives your greeting. *Fruit-Gathering.*

There is a land where no doubt and sorrow have rule: where the terror of death is no more. *Kabir's Poems.*

September 16

Goodness and love are infinite, and only in the infinite is the perfect realisation of freedom possible. *Sadhana.*

There is a secret joy in the bosom of the night. Let me fill my heart with it and carry it through the day. *Crossing.*

I do not know other things about God, but I know this, Thou art my Father. *Personality.*

September 17

Friend, you have come to me like the first sudden breeze of spring. *Sacrifice.*

I have your promise that my portion of the best in this world will come from your hands. *Fruit-Gathering.*

A truth opens up the whole horizon; it leads us to the Infinite. *Sadhana.*

September 18

September 19

September 20

September 18

The lover seeks his own other self in the beloved.
Sadhana.

Your songs, like birds from the lonely land of snow, are winging to build their nests in my heart against the warmth of its April, and I am content to wait for the merry season. *Fruit-Gathering.*

The night kisses the fading day whispering to his ear, 'I am death, your mother. I am to give you fresh birth.'
Stray Birds.

September 19

Man in his rôle of a creator is ever creating forms, and they come out of his abounding joy. *Sadhana.*

O God, my Father, the world of sins remove from me.
Personality.

Dear friend, I feel the silence of your great thoughts of many a deepening eventide on this beach when I listen to these waves. *Stray Birds.*

September 20

Love is perfection of consciousness. *Sadhana*

At his breath the flower spreads its wings and flutters in the wind. *Fruit-Gathering.*

I feel thy beauty, dark night, like that of the loved woman when she has put out the lamp. *Stray Birds.*

September 21

September 22

September 23

September 21

A mere token is of permanent worth to us when we have love in our heart. *Sadhana.*

Thou hast made me endless, such is thy pleasure. *Gitanjali.*

I fear to be led by others, lest I miss you waiting in some road corner to be my guide. *Fruit-Gathering.*

September 22

The human soul is on its journey from law to love, from discipline to liberation, from the moral plane to the spiritual. *Sadhana.*

This frail vessel thou emptiest again and again, and fillest it ever with fresh life. *Gitanjali.*

Wherever there is something which is concretely personal and human, there is woman's world. *Personality.*

September 23

Love is the ultimate meaning of everything around us. *Sadhana.*

Thy infinite gifts come to me only on those very small hands of mine.

Ages pass, and still thou pourest, and still there is room to fill. *Gitanjali.*

Not hammer-strokes, but dance of the water sings the pebbles into perfection. *Stray Birds.*

SEPTEMBER 24

SEPTEMBER 25

SEPTEMBER 26

September 24

The night shall wane, the darkness shall vanish,
Have faith, brave heart. *Sadhana.*

When thou commandest me to sing it seems that my heart would break with pride; and I look to thy face, and tears come to my eyes. *Gitanjali.*

My Lord brings to me words of sorrow and words of joy, and he himself heals their strife. *Kabir's Poems.*

September 25

Man's abiding happiness is not in getting anything, but in giving himself up to what is greater than himself. *Sadhana.*

All that is harsh and dissonant in my life melts into one sweet harmony—and my adoration spreads wings like a glad bird on its flight across the sea. *Gitanjali.*

To be outspoken is easy when you do not wait to speak the complete truth. *Stray Birds*

September 26

Wake up from sleep, from the languor of despair; receive the light of new dawn with a song. *Sadhana.*

The light of thy music illumines the world. *Gitanjali.*

Love truly by not making your love extravagant: for truth can afford to be simple. *Sacrifice.*

September 27

September 28

September 29

September 27

I know thou takest pleasure in my singing. I know that only as a singer I come before thy presence.

Gitanjali.

This rainy evening the wind is restless.
I look at the swaying branches and ponder over the greatness of all things. *Stray Birds.*

More than all else do I cherish at heart that love which makes me to live a limitless life in this world.

Kabir's Poems.

September 28

When our whole mind is bent only upon making use of this world, it loses for us its true value. *Sadhana.*

I touch by the edge of the far-spreading wing of my song thy feet which I never could aspire to reach.

Gitanjali.

All our spiritual teachers have proclaimed the infinite worth of the individual. *Personality.*

September 29

Intellect sets us apart from the things to be known, but love knows its object by fusion. *Sadhana.*

The human world is the woman's world, be it domestic or be it full of the other activities of life which are human activities. *Personality.*

The shadows of evening fall thick and deep.
Open your window to the West, and be lost in the sky of love. *Kabir's Poems.*

September 30

SEPTEMBER 30

Here rolls the sea, and even here lies the other shore waiting to be reached—yes, here is this everlasting present, not distant, not anywhere else. *Sadhana.*

The life breath of thy music runs from sky to sky. *Gitanjali.*

You had sweet shyness in your eyelids, like a dewdrop on the tip of a flower-petal. *Sacrifice.*

AUTUMN

THE evening beckons, and I would fain follow the travellers who sailed in the last ferry of the ebb-tide to cross the dark.

Some were for home, some for the farther shore, yet all have ventured to sail.

But I sit alone at the landing, having left my home and missed the boat : summer is gone and my winter's harvest is lost.

I wait for that love which gathers failures to sow them in tears on the dark, that they may bear fruit when day rises anew.

Fugitive.

ACCEPT me, my Lord, accept me for this while.

Let those orphaned days which passed without thee be forgotten.

Only spread this little moment wide across thy lap, holding it under thy light.

I have wandered in pursuit of voices that drew me yet led me nowhere.

Now let me sit in peace and listen to thy words in the soul of thy silence.

Crossing.

OCTOBER 1

OCTOBER 2

October 1

The joy which is without form must create, must translate itself into form. *Sadhana.*

Life of my life, I shall ever try to keep my body pure, knowing that thy living touch is upon all my limbs. *Gitanjali.*

Let me think that there is one among those stars that guides my life through the dark unknown. *Stray Birds.*

October 2

By the very act of possession, we know that we are greater than the things we possess. *Sadhana.*

Thou hast made my heart captive in the endless meshes of thy music, my Master! *Gitanjali.*

Woman, with the grace of your fingers you touched my things, and order came out like music. *Stray Birds.*

October 3

October 4

October 5

October 3

In all our deeper love, getting and non-getting run ever parallel. *Sadhana.*

The holy stream of thy music breaks through all stony obstacles and rushes on. *Gitanjali.*

You have won my heart, and my heart is ready to offer you its best treasure. *Sacrifice.*

October 4

Man must realise the wholeness of his existence, his place in the infinite. *Sadhana.*

I shall ever try to keep all untruths out from my thoughts, knowing that thou art that truth which has kindled the light of reason in my mind. *Gitanjali.*

The dust of the dead words clings to thee.
Wash thy soul with silence. *Stray Birds.*

October 5

Love is the one living truth that makes all realities true. *Sadhana.*

My thoughts shimmer with these shimmering leaves, and my heart sings with the touch of this sunlight; my life is glad to be floating with all things into the blue of space, into the dark of time. *Stray Birds.*

I shall ever try to drive all evils away from my heart and keep my love in flower, knowing that thou hast thy seat in the inmost shrine of my heart. *Gitanjali.*

October 6

October 7

October 8

October 6

Man's history is the history of his journey to the unknown in quest of the realisation of his immortal self, his soul. *Sadhana.*

When grace is lost from life, come with a burst of song. *Gitanjali.*

When we rejoice in our fullness, then we can part with our fruits with joy. *Stray Birds.*

October 7

The night is dark, and your slumber is deep in the hush of my being. Wake, O pain of love, for I know not how to open the door. *Fruit-Gathering.*

It shall be my endeavour to reveal thee in my actions, knowing it is thy power gives me strength to act.

Gitanjali.

Will has its supreme response, not in the world of law, but in the world of freedom. *Personality.*

October 8

I felt I saw your face, and I launched my boat in the dark. *Crossing.*

Pluck this little flower, and take it, delay not!
I fear lest it droop and drop into the dust.

Gitanjali.

Love! when you come with the burning lamp of pain in your hand, I can see your face and know you as bliss.

Stray Birds.

OCTOBER 9

OCTOBER 10

OCTOBER 11

October 9

Honour the flower with a touch of pain from thy hand and pluck it. *Gitanjali.*

Thoughts pass in my mind like flocks of ducks in the sky.
I hear the voice of their wings. *Stray Birds.*

Comrade of the road, here are my traveller's greetings to thee. *Crossing.*

October 10

Man has to discover that accumulation is not realisation. It is the inner light that reveals him, not outer things. *Sadhana.*

Let me make my life simple and straight, like a flute of reed for thee to fill with music. *Gitanjali.*

The world has kissed my soul with its pain, asking for its return in songs. *Stray Birds.*

October 11

It is the self of man which the great King of the universe has not shadowed with his throne—he has left it free. *Sadhana.*

Accept only what is offered by sacred love. *Gitanjali.*

I have dipped the vessel of my heart into this silent hour; it has filled with love. *Stray Birds.*

OCTOBER 12

OCTOBER 13

OCTOBER 14

October 12

My heart can never find its way to where thou keepest company with the companionless among the poorest, the lowliest and the lost. *Gitanjali.*

The clouds fill the watercups of the river, hiding themselves in the distant hills. *Stray Birds.*

Put out the lamps, my heart, the lamps of the lonely night.
The call comes to open your doors, for the morning light is abroad. *Crossing.*

October 13

Is your heart lost to the Lover calling you across his immeasurable loneliness? *Fugitive.*

Wake, Love, wake! brim my empty cup, and with a breath of song ruffle the night. *Fruit-Gathering.*

God is the joy which reveals itself in forms.
It is his will which creates. *Personality.*

October 14

Man's freedom is never in being saved troubles, but it is the freedom to take trouble for his own good. *Sadhana.*

Our master himself has joyfully taken upon him the bonds of creation; he is bound with us all for ever. *Gitanjali.*

I spill water from my water jar as I walk on my way.
Very little remains for my home. *Stray Birds.*

OCTOBER 15

OCTOBER 16

OCTOBER 17

October 15

The universal is ever seeking its consummation in the unique. *Sadhana.*

The traveller has to knock at every alien door to come to his own, and one has to wander through all the outer worlds to reach the innermost shrine at the end. *Gitanjali.*

Your smile was the flowers of your own fields, your talk was the rustle of your own mountain pines, but your heart was the woman that we all know. *Stray Birds.*

October 16

It is our joy of the infinite in us that gives us our joy in ourselves. *Sadhana.*

I live in the hope of meeting with him. *Gitanjali.*

The sunshine greets me with a smile.
The rain, his sad sister, talks to my heart. *Stray Birds.*

October 17

Day by day thou art making me worthy of thy full acceptance by refusing me ever and anon. *Gitanjali.*

My flower of the day dropped its petals forgotten.
In the evening it ripens into a golden fruit of memory. *Stray Birds.*

There is a secret joy in the bosom of the night.
Let me fill my heart with it and carry it through the day. *Crossing.*

October 18

October 19

October 20

October 18

I am like the road in the night listening to the footfalls of its memories in silence. *Stray Birds.*

From the heart of the fathomless blue comes one golden call and across the dusk of tears I try to gaze at thy face. *Crossing.*

Only the radiance of Truth shines in my Lord's Durbar. *Kabir's Poems.*

October 19

If thou showest me not thy face, if thou leavest me wholly aside, I know not how I am to pass these long, rainy hours. *Gitanjali.*

The evening sky to me is like a window, and a lighted lamp, and a waiting behind it. *Stray Birds.*

Thy word has rent night's veils, the buds of the morning are opened. *Crossing.*

October 20

Make me thy poet, O Night!
There are some who have sat speechless for ages in thy shadow; let me utter their songs. *Fruit-Gathering.*

I keep gazing on the far-away gloom of the sky, and my heart wanders wailing with the restless wind. *Gitanjali.*

He who is too busy doing good finds no time to be good. *Stray Birds.*

October 21

October 22

October 23

October 21

I will meet one day the Life within me, the joy that hides in my life. *Fruit-Gathering.*

The morning will surely come, the darkness will vanish, and thy voice pour down in golden streams breaking through the sky. *Gitanjali.*

I am the autumn cloud, empty of rain.
See my fullness in the field of ripened rice.
Stray Birds.

October 22

The poet's mind floats and dances on the waves of life amidst the voices of wind and water. *Fruit-Gathering.*

Thy words will take wing in songs from every one of my birds' nests, and thy melodies will break forth in flowers in all my forest groves. *Gitanjali.*

Those who pursue the knowledge of the finite for its own sake cannot find truth. *Personality.*

October 23

The bird of the morning sings.
Whence has he word of the morning before the morning breaks, and when the dragon Night still holds the sky in its cold black coils? *Fruit-Gathering.*

That vague sweetness made my heart ache with longing, and it seemed to me that it was the eager breath of the summer seeking for its completion. *Gitanjali.*

Our soul is nourished only through the good, which is the recognition of its inner kinship. *Sadhana.*

October 24

October 25

October 26

October 24

Tell me, bird of the morning, how, through the two-fold night of the sky and the leaves, he found his way into your dream, the messenger out of the East?

Fruit-Gathering.

Do you not feel a thrill passing through the air with the notes of the far-away song floating from the other shore. *Gitanjali.*

The infinite and finite are one, as the song and the singing are one. *Personality.*

October 25

Bare your forehead, waiting for the first blessing of light, and sing with the bird of the morning in glad faith.

Fruit-Gathering.

Thou art the solitary wayfarer in this deserted street.

Oh, my only friend, the gates are open in my house—do not pass by like a dream. *Gitanjali.*

Let me not put myself wrongly to my world and set it against me. *Stray Birds.*

October 26

Master, give me the least fraction of the wealth that disdains all the wealth of the world. *Fruit-Gathering.*

Art thou abroad on this stormy night on thy journey of love, my friend? *Gitanjali.*

Darkness travels towards the light. *Stray Birds.*

OCTOBER 27

OCTOBER 28

OCTOBER 29

October 27

By what dim shore of the ink-black river art thou treading thy course to come to me, my friend?

Gitanjali.

Let my doing nothing, when I have nothing to do, become untroubled in its depth of peace, like the evening on the seashore when the water is silent. *Stray Birds.*

O my heart, how could you turn from the smile of your Lord, and wander so far from him? *Kabir's Poems.*

October 28

The Unknown is the perpetual freedom.

Fruit-Gathering.

It is thou who drawest the veil of night upon the tired eyes of the day to renew its sight in a fresher gladness of awakening. *Gitanjali.*

My sad thoughts tease me asking me their own names.

Stray Birds.

October 29

Open the inner door of the shrine, light the candle, and let us meet there in silence before our God.

Fruit-Gathering.

He came when the night was still; he had his harp in his hands, and my dreams became resonant with its melodies. *Gitanjali.*

I shall die again and again to know that life is inexhaustible. *Stray Birds.*

October 30

October 31

OCTOBER 30

I started up from my dream and felt a sweet trace of a strange fragrance in the south wind. *Gitanjali.*

The waning night lingers at my doors, let her take her leave in songs. *Fruit-Gathering.*

When I stand before thee at the day's end, thou shalt see my scars and know that I had my wounds and also my healing. *Stray Birds.*

OCTOBER 31

Pour your heart into my life strings, my Master, in tunes that descend from your stars. *Fruit-Gathering.*

I will keep still and wait like the night with starry vigil and its head bent low with patience. *Gitanjali.*

Some day I shall sing to thee in the sunrise of some other world, 'I have seen thee before in the light of the earth, in the love of man'. *Stray Birds.*

NOVEMBER

My heart, the bird of the wilderness, has found its sky in your eyes.

They are the cradle of the morning, they are the kingdom of the stars.

My songs are lost in their depths.

Let me but soar in that sky, in its lonely immensity.

Let me but cleave its clouds and spread wings in its sunshine. *Gardener.*

NOVEMBER 1

NOVEMBER 2

November 1

Before I go, may I linger over my last refrain, completing its music, may the lamp be lit to see your face, and the wreath woven to crown you. *Fruit-Gathering.*

The storm of the last night has crowned this morning with golden peace. *Stray Birds.*

The reality of the eternal is there, where it contains all times within itself. *Personality.*

November 2

What music is that in whose measure the world is rocked? *Fruit-Gathering.*

By all means they try to hold me secure who love me in this world. But it is otherwise with thy love, which is greater than theirs, and thou keepest me free. *Gitanjali.*

Clouds come floating into my life from other days no longer to shed rain or usher storm, but to give colour to my sunset sky. *Stray Birds.*

NOVEMBER 3

NOVEMBER 4

NOVEMBER 5

November 3

Let only that little be left of my will whereby I may feel thee on every side, and come to thee in everything, and offer to thee my love every moment. *Gitanjali.*

Truth seems to come with its final word ; and the final word gives birth to its next. *Stray Birds.*

Within this earthen vessel the Eternal soundeth, and the spring wells up. *Kabir's Poems.*

November 4

I have kissed this world with my eyes and my limbs ; I have wrapt it within my heart in numberless folds ; I have flooded its days and nights with thoughts till the world and my life have grown one.

Fruit-Gathering.

Let only that little of my fetters be left whereby I am bound with thy will, and thy purpose is carried out in my life—and that is the fetter of thy love. *Gitanjali.*

I wait for that love which gathers failures to sow them in tears. *Fugitive.*

November 5

I love my life because I love the light of the sky so enwoven with me. *Fruit-Gathering.*

Give me the strength lightly to bear my joys and sorrows. *Gitanjali..*

I have met thee, where the light startles the darkness into dawn. *Crossing.*

T

November 6

November 7

November 8

November 6

Thy will knows no end in me: where the old tracks are lost, new country is revealed with its wonders.

Gitanjali.

There are tracts in my life that are bare and silent. They are the open spaces where my busy days had their light and air. *Stray Birds.*

Someone has secretly left in my heart a flower of love.

Crossing.

November 7

Your fleeting steps kiss the dust of this world into sweetness, sweeping aside all waste. *Fugitive.*

That I want thee, only thee—let my heart repeat without end. *Gitanjali.*

In my heart is my Lord, one with me.

Fruit-Gathering.

November 8

My thoughts are quickened by this rhythm of unseen feet round which the anklets of light are shaken.

Fugitive.

As the night keeps hidden in its gloom the petition for light, even thus in the depth of my unconsciousness rings the cry—I want thee. *Gitanjali.*

In her, the Eternal One breaks in two in a joy that no longer may contain itself, and overflows in the pain of love. *Fruit-Gathering.*

November 9

November 10

November 11

November 9

I hear the thundering flood tumbling my life from world to world and form to form, scattering my being in an endless spray of gifts, in sorrowings and songs. *Fugitive.*

When tumultuous work raises its din on all sides, shutting me out from beyond, come to me, my lord of silence, with thy peace and rest. *Gitanjali.*

You came for a moment to my side, and touched me with the great mystery of the woman that there is in the heart of creation. *Fruit-Gathering.*

November 10

The tide runs high, the wind blows, the boat dances like thine own desire, my heart! *Fugitive.*

When my beggarly heart sits crouched, shut up in a corner, break open the door, my king, and come with the ceremony of a king. *Gitanjali.*

Yours is the heaven that lies in the common dust, and you are there for me, you are there for all.
Fruit-Gathering.

November 11

Leave the hoard on the shore, and sail over the unfathomed dark towards limitless light. *Fugitive.*

Let the cloud of grace bend low from above like the tearful look of the mother on the day of the father's wrath.
Gitanjali.

Light's greeting spreads from the East to the West.
Crossing.

NOVEMBER 12

NOVEMBER 13

NOVEMBER 14

November 12

I shall follow wind and cloud; I shall follow the stars to where day breaks behind the hills; I shall follow lovers who, as they walk, twine their days into a wreath on a single thread of song, 'I love'. *Fugitive.*

I sit on the grass and gaze upon the sky, and dream of the sudden splendour of Thy coming. *Gitanjali.*

The spring breeze has overheard your desire, the day will not end before you have fulfilled your being.
Fruit-Gathering.

November 13

The trees hang vaguely over the bank, and the land appears as though it already belonged to the past. *Fugitive.*

Entering my heart unbidden, even as one of the common crowd, unknown to me, my king, thou didst press the signet of eternity upon many a fleeting moment of my life.
Gitanjali.

Your bonds will burst, the bud will open into flower, and when you die in the fullness of life, even then the spring will live on. *Fruit-Gathering.*

November 14

O that I were stored with a secret, like unshed rain in summer clouds—a secret, folded up in silence, that I could wander away with. *Fugitive.*

Thou didst not turn in contempt from my childish play among dust, and the steps that I heard in my playroom are the same that are echoing from star to star.
Gitanjali.

Let us live. Let us have the true joy of life, which is the joy of the poet in pouring himself out in his poems.
Personality.

November 15

November 16

November 17

November 15

O that I had someone to whisper to, where slow waters lap under trees that doze in the sun. *Fugitive.*

From dawn till dusk I sit here before my door, and I know that of a sudden the happy moment will arrive when I shall see. *Gitanjali.*

Send me the love which is cool and pure like your rain that blesses the thirsty earth and fills the homely earthen jars. *Fruit-Gathering.*

November 16

The hush this evening seems to expect a footfall, and you ask me for the cause of my tears. *Fugitive.*

This is my delight, thus to wait and watch at the wayside where shadow chases light and the rain comes in the wake of the summer. *Gitanjali.*

The waves of my tunes wash your feet, but I know not how to reach them. *Fruit-Gathering.*

November 17

Many a song have I sung in many a mood of mind, but all their notes have always proclaimed, 'He comes, comes, ever comes'. *Gitanjali.*

Send me the love that would soak down into the centre of being, and from there would spread like the unseen sap through the branching tree of life, giving birth to fruits and flowers. *Fruit-Gathering.*

Behold, what wonderful rest is in the Supreme Spirit,
And he enjoys it who makes himself meet for it.

Kabir's Poems.

November 18

November 19

November 20

November 18

Long have you watched over the store gathered by weary years. Let it be stripped, with nothing remaining but the desolate triumph of losing all. *Fugitive.*

It is the golden touch of his feet that makes my joy to shine. *Gitanjali.*

This life of ours has been filled with the gifts of the Divine Giver. *Personality.*

November 19

I know not why to-day my life is all astir, and a feeling of tremulous joy is passing through my heart.

Gitanjali.

You sang to me in the ecstasies of my life and I forgot to sing to you. *Fruit-Gathering.*

Held by the cords of love, the swing of the Ocean of Joy sways to and fro :
And a mighty sound breaks forth in song.

Kabir's Poems.

November 20

Let him appear before my sight as the first of all lights and all forms ; the first thrill of joy to my awakened soul let it come from his glance. And let my return to myself be immediate return to him. *Gitanjali.*

You were the inmost joy in the play of my youth, and when I was too busy with the play the joy was passed by.

Fruit-Gathering.

The whole world does its works and commits its errors :
But few are the lovers who know the Beloved.

Kabir's Poems.

November 21

November 22

November 23

November 21

From the heart of the fathomless blue comes one golden call. *Crossing.*

The morning sea of silence broke into ripples of bird songs; and the flowers were all merry by the roadside; and the wealth of gold was scattered through the rift of the clouds. *Gitanjali.*

Are those your songs that are echoing in the dark caves of my being? *Fruit-Gathering.*

November 22

What gifts have you brought in both hands to fling before me in the dust? *Fugitive.*

One plaintive little strain mingled with the great music of the world, and with a flower for a prize you came down. *Gitanjali.*

You love to discover that I love this world where you have brought me. *Fruit-Gathering.*

November 23

From now there shall be no fear left for me in this world, and thou shalt be victorious in all my strife. *Gitanjali.*

I sat alone in a corner of my house thinking it too narrow for any guest, but now when its door is flung open by an unbidden joy I find there is room for thee and for all the world. *Fruit-Gathering.*

My love for her is my life flowing in its fullness, like a river in autumn flood. *Lover's Gift.*

NOVEMBER 24

NOVEMBER 25

NOVEMBER 26

November 24

Who can imagine that aching overflow of splendour which created you! *Fugitive.*

Thou hast taken me as thy partner of all this wealth. In my heart is the endless play of thy delight. In my life thy will is ever taking shape. *Gitanjali.*

Day after day you buy your sunrise from my heart, and you find your love carven into the image of my life. *Fruit-Gathering.*

November 25

Be content if the music is true, though the words are not to be believed. *Fugitive.*

Thou who art the King of kings hast decked thyself in beauty to captivate my heart. *Gitanjali.*

To the birds you gave songs, the birds gave you songs in return. *Fruit-Gathering.*

November 26

Life is perpetual creation: it has truth when it outgrows itself in the infinite. *Personality.*

Thy love loses itself in the love of thy lover, and there art thou seen in the perfect union of two. *Gitanjali.*

My love, I will keep you hidden in my eyes. *Fugitive.*

November 27

November 28

November 29

November 27

For me the sun of fulfilment has risen, and the stars have faded in its light. I have mastered the knowledge which gives life. *Fugitive.*

The light strikes, my darling, the chords of my love; the sky opens, the wind runs wild, laughter passes over the earth. *Gitanjali.*

You made your winds light, and they are fleet in your service. You burdened my hands that I myself may lighten them. *Fruit-Gathering.*

November 28

Let me hold my head high in the courage and pride of being your servant. *Fruit-Gathering.*

Proudly step into my orchard, my queen, sit there in the shade, pluck the ripe fruits from their stems. *Lover's Gift.*

When I go from hence let this be my passing word, that what I have seen is unsurpassable. *Gitanjali.*

November 29

Thy face is bent from above, thine eyes look down on my eyes, and my heart has touched thy feet. *Gitanjali.*

You created your Earth filling its shadows with fragments of light.

There you paused; you left me empty-handed in the dust to create your heaven. *Fruit-Gathering.*

The building of man's true world,—the living world of truth and beauty—is the function of Art. *Personality.*

November 30

November 30

Friend, you cannot now escape, for your secret is mine.

Fugitive.

Pearl fishers dive for pearls, merchants sail in their ships, while children gather pebbles and scatter them again.

Gitanjali.

I came and your heart heaved; pain came to you and joy.

You touched me and tingled into love.

Fruit-Gathering.

DECEMBER

We came hither together, friend, and now at the cross-roads I stop to bid you farewell.

Your path is wide and straight before you, but my call comes up by ways from the unknown.

I shall follow wind and cloud : I shall follow the stars to where day breaks behind the hills : I shall follow lovers who, as they walk, twine their days into a wreath on a single thread of song, 'I love'. *Fugitive.*

December 1

December 2

December 1

Day after day, in raising your head, in a glance, in the motion of your hands, your love spoke as the sea speaks through its waves. *Fugitive.*

The sea plays with children, and pale gleams the smile of the sea beach. *Gitanjali.*

Your world is a branching spray of light filling your hands, but your heaven is in my secret heart; it slowly opens its buds in shy love. *Fruit-Gathering.*

December 2

On a sudden my voice would send your heart quivering through your limbs—have I never witnessed it? *Fugitive.*

The sleep that flits on baby's eyes—does anybody know from where it comes? *Gitanjali.*

Keep me at your door ever attending to your wishes, and let me go about in your Kingdom accepting your call. *Fruit-Gathering.*

December 3

December 4

December 5

DECEMBER 3

What made you sit by me on the grass and sing songs you brought hither from the assembly of the stars, while darkness stooped over the river bank as love droops over its own sad silence? *Fugitive.*

There is a rumour that a young pale beam of a crescent moon touched the edge of a vanishing autumn cloud—and there was born the smile that flickers on baby's lips when he sleeps. *Gitanjali.*

When Man bursts his mortal bounds, is not the boundless revealed that moment? *Fruit-Gathering.*

DECEMBER 4

You have been in my heart ever since I was a child. *Fugitive.*

Put out your hand through the night, let me hold it and fill it and keep it: let me feel its touch along the lengthening stretch of my loneliness. *Fruit-Gathering.*

What is it in man that asserts its immortality in spite of the fact of death? *Personality.*

DECEMBER 5

The relation of understanding is partial, but the relation of love is complete. *Sadhana.*

When I sing to make you dance, my child, I truly know why there is music in leaves, and why waves send their chorus of voices to the heart of the listening earth—when I sing to make you dance. *Gitanjali.*

When you have finished with others, that is my time. I come to ask what remains for your last servant to do. *Gardener.*

December 6

December 7

December 8

December 6

We must not slay our souls. We must not forget that life is here to express the eternal in us. *Personality.*

I watch if young straying hearts meet together, and two pairs of eager eyes beg for music to break their silence and speak for them. *Gardener.*

The whole earth and infinite space are for the child, for the New Life. *Fugitive.*

December 7

Thou hast made me known to friends whom I knew not. Thou hast given me seats in homes not my own. *Gitanjali.*

Our freedom as a creator finds its highest joy in contributing its own voice to the concert of the world-music. *Personality.*

I know well the rhythm of your steps, they are beating in my heart. *Gardener.*

December 8

The old abides in the new, and there also thou abidest. *Gitanjali.*

A child running laughing from its mother's arms into the open light.

'Was it only for this that they said it was the day of the Coming?'

'Yes, this was why they said there was music in the air and light in the sky.' *Fugitive.*

One day with fresh wonder you came into my life that was fluttered with its first love. *Lover's Gift.*

December 9

December 10

December 11

December 9

Wherever thou leadest me it is thou who ever linkest my heart with bonds of joy to the unfamiliar.

Gitanjali.

I feel my body vanishing into the dust whereon my beloved walks. *Fugitive.*

When I sit and listen for his footsteps, leaves do not rustle on the trees, and the water is still in the river. It is my own heart that beats wildly—I do not know how to quiet it. *Gardener.*

December 10

When one knows Thee, then alien there is none, then no door is shut. *Gitanjali.*

My heart melts in the light and merges in the mirror whereby he views his face. *Fugitive.*

I stand aside in the shade under the tree with my head bent in the calm of the dawn by the lonely road to the temple. *Lover's Gift.*

December 11

I have come to dedicate my lamp to the sky.

Gitanjali.

My love, I will keep you hidden in my eyes; I will thread your image like a gem on my joy and hang it on my bosom. *Fugitive.*

When my love comes and sits by my side, the night darkens, the wind blows out the lamp, and the clouds draw veils over the stars. It is the jewel at my own breast that shines and gives light. I do not know how to hide it.

Gardener.

December 12

December 13

December 14

December 18

Thou ever pourest for me the fresh draught of thy wine of various colours and fragrance, filling this earthen vessel to the brim. *Gitanjali.*

You have made me great with your love though I am but one among the many, drifting in the common tide. *Fugitive.*

The jasmine wreath that you wove me thrills to my heart like praise. *Gardener.*

December 19

No, I will never shut the doors of my senses. The delights of sight and hearing and touch will bear thy delight. *Gitanjali.*

He is not content with giving us himself, but he gives us strength that we may likewise give ourselves. *Sadhana.*

Suffering has driven man with his prayer to knock at the gate of the infinite. *Personality.*

December 20

Thy gifts to us mortals fulfil all our needs and yet run back to thee undiminished. *Gitanjali.*

Know that to-morrow's songs are in bud to-day, and should they see you walk by they would strain to breaking their immature hearts. *Fugitive.*

God's life flowing in its outpour of self-giving has touched man's life which is also abroad in its career of freedom. *Personality.*

DECEMBER 21

DECEMBER 22

DECEMBER 23

December 21

In the deepest silence of night the stars smile and whisper among themselves—'Unbroken perfection is over all'. *Gitanjali.*

Let my heart touch yours and kiss the pain out of your silence. *Fugitive.*

From the unknown island of a heart came a sudden warm breath of spring.

It fell upon my heart like a sigh of her body and whisper of her heart. *Gardener.*

December 22

Take this fleeting emptiness of mine, O my sun ever-glorious, paint it with colours, gild it with gold, float it on the wanton wind and spread it in varied wonders. *Gitanjali.*

The night has thrown up from its depth this little hour, that love may build a new world within these shut doors, to be lighted by this solitary lamp. *Fugitive.*

Do not keep to yourself the secret of your heart, my friend! Say it to me, only to me, in secret. *Gardener.*

December 23

The Great is a born child. *Stray Birds.*

God has sent woman to love the world, which is a world of ordinary things and events. *Personality.*

You who smile so gently, softly whisper; my heart will hear it, not my ears. *Gardener.*

December 24

December 25

December 26

December 24

It is not enough that I am given to my love once and for ever, but out of that I must fashion new gifts every day. *Fugitive.*

His joy is ever dedicating itself in the dedication which is His creation. *Sadhana.*

The one cry of the personal man has been to know the Supreme Person. *Personality.*

December 25

'What does the child bring to you?'
'Hope for all the world and its joy.' *Fugitive.*

Here is thy footstool and there rest thy feet, where are the poorest and the lowliest and the lost. *Gitanjali.*

God is giving himself in love to all. *Personality.*

December 26

When I bring my sorrow to thee as my offering, thou rewardest me with thy grace. *Gitanjali.*

I was speaking to you, my love, with mind barely conscious of my voice—tell me, had it any meaning? Did it bring you any message from beyond life's borders? *Fugitive.*

Speak to me, my love! Tell me in words what you sang.
The night is dark. The stars are lost in clouds. The wind is sighing through the leaves. *Gardener.*

December 27

December 28

December 29

December 27

I have wandered in pursuit of voices that drew me, yet led me nowhere.

Now let me sit and listen to thy words in the soul of my silence. *Crossing.*

When we two first met, my heart rang out in music, ' She, who is eternally afar, is beside you for ever '. *Fugitive.*

You are the evening cloud floating in the sky of my dreams. *Gardener.*

December 28

I stand under the golden canopy of thine evening sky and I lift my eager eyes to thy face. *Gitanjali.*

Wake up, my song, from thy languor, rend this screen of the familiar, and fly to my beloved there, in the endless surprise of our first meeting ! *Fugitive.*

I have caught you, and wrapt you, my love, in the net of my music. *Gardener.*

December 29

Make me thy cup, and let my fullness be for thee and thine. *Stray Birds.*

Your desires come from the hive of the past to haunt my heart, and I sit still to listen to their wings. *Fugitive.*

Oh, my only friend, my best beloved, the gates are all open in my house—do not pass by like a dream. *Gitanjali.*

December 30

December 31

December 30

I have come to the brink of eternity from which nothing can vanish. *Gitanjali.*

I speak truth; for I have accepted truth in life, and have swept all tinsels away. *Kabir's Poems.*

The Great Master plays: the breath is his own, but the instrument is our mind, through which he brings out his songs of creation. *Personality.*

December 31

When there was light in my world you stood outside my eyes. Now that there is none, you come into my heart. *Cycle of Spring.*

Someone has stolen my heart and scattered it abroad in the sky. *Crossing.*

The spring days come again time after time; the full moon takes leave and comes on another visit; the flowers come again and blush upon their branches year after year; and it is likely that I take my leave only to come to you again. *Gardener.*

SALUTATION

In one salutation to thee, my God, let all my senses spread out and touch this world at thy feet.

Like a rain cloud of July hung low with its burden of unshed showers let all my mind bend down at thy door in one salutation to thee.

Let all my songs gather together their diverse strains into a single current and flow to a sea of silence in one salutation to thee.

Like a flock of home-sick cranes flying night and day back to their mountain nests let all my life take its voyage to its eternal home in one salutation to thee.

Gitanjali.

FAREWELL

PEACE, my heart, let the time for the parting be sweet.

Let it not be a death but completeness.

Let love melt into memory and pain into songs.

Let the flight in the sky end in the folding up of the wings over the nest.

Let the last touch of your hands be gentle like the flower of the night.

Stand still, O Beautiful End, for a moment, and say your last words in silence.

I bow to you and hold up my lamp to light you on your way.

Gardener.